8.08

D1060538

prognosis in functional psychoses

Publication Number 496
AMERICAN LECTURE SERIES®

A Monograph in
The BANNERSTONE DIVISION *of*
AMERICAN LECTURES IN OBJECTIVE PSYCHIATRY

Edited by
WILLIAM HORSLEY GANTT, M.D.
Director, Pavlovian Laboratory
The Johns Hopkins University
Baltimore, Maryland
and
Chief Scientist, V.A. Hospital
Perry Point, Maryland

prognosis in
functional psychoses

CLINICAL, SOCIAL AND GENETIC ASPECTS

By

CHRISTIAN ASTRUP, M.D.
The Pavlovian Laboratory
The Johns Hopkins University
Baltimore, Maryland
Formerly, Gaustad Hospital
Oslo, Norway

ARNE FOSSUM, M.D.
Gaustad Hospital, Oslo, Norway

ROLF HOLMBOE, M.D.
Gaustad Hospital, Oslo, Norway

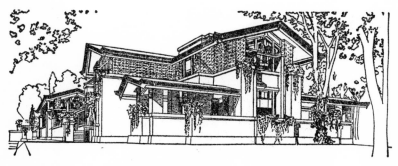

CHARLES C THOMAS • **PUBLISHER**
Springfield • *Illinois* • *U.S.A.*

Published and Distributed Throughout the World by
CHARLES C THOMAS • PUBLISHER
BANNERSTONE HOUSE
301-327 East Lawrence Avenue, Springfield, Illinois, U.S.A.

*With THOMAS BOOKS careful attention is given to all details of
manufacturing and design. It is the Publisher's desire to present books
that are satisfactory as to their physical qualities and artistic possibilities
and appropriate for their particular use. THOMAS BOOKS will be true
to those laws of quality that assure a good name and good will.*

Printed in the United States of America

Dedicated
to
our teacher
Örnulv Ödegård,
pioneer in the field
of
social psychiatry

INTRODUCTION

The present publication surveys the results of a follow-up study of 1,102 functional psychoses treated in Gaustad Hospital. All first admissions of functional psychotics from 1938 to 1950 have been included in the material. We have unselected samples of all types of such conditions. For the clinical analysis of case histories it was a great advantage that Professor *Ödegård* was the chief of the hospital during the whole period. The case histories are rather uniform and practically all patients have been seen by him.

In previous publications we have analyzed the acute schizophrenics and schizophreniform psychotics (68) as well as acute affective psychoses (8). Reference is made to a great extent to these previous studies, partly for comparisons and partly in order to avoid unnecessary repetition.

Several comparisons have also been made with a sample of 484 schizophrenics and schizophreniform psychotic who were clinically analyzed in the same way as the follow-up cases and experimentally investigated by *Astrup* with conditional reflex methods (9).

The purpose of our investigation was to make multifactorial analysis of prognostic, clinical, social, hereditary and physiological aspects of various types of functional psychoses.

ACKNOWLEDGMENTS

These investigations could not have been carried out without the financial support given by the Norwegian Research Council for Science and the Humanities, to whom we are deeply grateful.

We also want to thank Professor Örnulv Ödegård and Dr. Johan Bremer for their stimulating interest and valuable aid.

We would express our profound gratitude to William Horsley Gantt, Maria Simonson and Priscilla Alden Beach for their help with editing the book.

C. A.
A. F.
R. H.

CONTENTS

Contents

LIST OF TABLES

prognosis in functional psychoses

Chapter I

METHOD OF FOLLOW-UP INVESTIGATIONS

The follow-up studies were started at the end of 1955 and carried through during the years from 1956 to 1960. We started by sorting out from the national register of the insane all first admissions to Gaustad Hospital during the years 1938 to 1950 with a duration of illness of less than six months prior to admission.

Among these cases those with a diagnosis of schizophrenia or reactive psychoses with an admixture of schizophrenic symptoms were selected for the first follow-up project (68). The reactive psychoses without schizophrenic symptoms and cases diagnosed as manic-depressive were selected for the second follow-up project (8).

The national register of the insane had been very accurate in coding the duration of illness, as only in a few cases did our analysis of case histories show that the illness had actually lasted more than six months prior to admission. Upon sorting the remaining group of functional psychoses with a duration of illness of more than six months, again only a few were found to have lasted less than six months. The remaining group included some acute cases which originally were excluded for geographical and other reasons (68).

Altogether there were 1,102 first admissions of functional psychoses to Gaustad Hospital during the chosen period. A five-year follow-up period was considered as a minimum for estimating the long-term course of the illness.

For the clinical outcome the material was divided into the same main groups as in our previous follow-up studies (8, 68). We have three schizophrenic groups, deteriorated, improved and recovered. The affective psychoses were divided into reactive and manic-depressive groups.

3

In the analysis of the case histories, the same principles were used as described in our publication on acute schizophrenia and schizophreniform psychoses (68). It is stressed that there may be a tendency to evaluate identical symptoms in a different way according to outcome. To avoid this bias, the investigation was started by coding all clinical factors from the case histories before seeing the patients.

From case histories and the national register of the insane it was possible to sort out most patients who were in mental hospitals or under public care as insane in family care or nursing homes. The boarding out system of the insane plays an important role in Norway, and is described in some detail by *Wing* (170). Patients in public care are under the supervision of public health officers, who have given us information about the clinical conditions of the patient. For patients in mental hospitals other than Gaustad, we considered information from the hospital doctors as sufficient. We have re-examined personally all patients staying at Gaustad Hospital during the period of investigation.

When patients had been discharged from the hospital, we had to trace them through the local population registers. As Norway has a well-developed population registration, and as people know each other well in a sparsely populated country, we were able, in spite of considerable migration, to trace practically all. In several cases it was necessary to seek assistance from health insurance officers, the Salvation Army, or the police.

The traced patients were re-examined personally as far as was practicable. Because Norway is a country with difficult communications, we restricted the personal re-examination to eastern, south-eastern and southern Norway. With this geographical limitation we have covered an area up to 400 kilometers away from the hospital. Altogether we have traveled about 60,000 kilometers by road in order to be able to see the patients in their homes. A few of the personally re-examined patients have been seen by R. *Christensen* in connection with a follow-up of leucotomized patients (28). It was not considered necessary to look up these patients again. In most cases seen personally we also obtained information from relatives and other connections.

In an attempt to cover western and northern Norway questionnaires were sent to patients, relatives and public health officers. For patients deceased five years or more after hospital admission, the clinical state up to the time of death was ascertained by information from hospitals, public health officers and relatives.

Table 1 surveys the methods by which the various clinical outcome groups were investigated (see Table 1).

TABLE 1

Survey of Patients Followed-up Five Years or More

Outcome	Personally Examined at Home	Personally Examined in Gaustad Hospital	Information from Relatives and other Connections	Information from Hospitals	Information from Public Health Officers	Questionnaires Answered by Patients	Deceased After More than 5 Years	Total
Deteriorated schizophrenics	75	118	6	66	110	0	41	416
Improved schizophrenics	81	5	7	2	8	10	4	117
Recovered schizophrenics	91	5	12	1	9	9	4	131
Reactive psychoses	113	6	7	6	22	32	20	206
Manic-depressive psychoses	56	5	3	7	8	11	12	102
Total followed up for 5 years or more	416	139	35	82	157	62	81	972

From the table it is seen that the clinical outcome of deteriorated schizophrenics who were alive is based, except in a few cases, on personal re-examination or information from other doctors. There is every reason to consider the schizophrenic course of illness as ascertained.

Among the improved and recovered schizophrenics the majority have been personally re-examined. This is important, as it may often be difficult to decide whether the patient has recovered or presents slight personality changes characteristic of a schizophrenic psychotic residual. Information from public health officers, relatives, and others is probably more reliable than a questionnaire answered by the patient himself. The main reason for this is that patients with schizophrenic defects as a rule lack insight into their condition, whereas those who come into contact with them realize their abnormal traits.

In the schizophrenic group questionnaires were answered by only nineteen patients. In ten of these cases additional information came from public health officers. Questionnaires were sent to fifty-seven patients in the schizophrenic group. The few answers demonstrate clearly that if questionnaires were the sole method employed one would miss the majority of schizophrenics. The recovered may answer, but those with schizophrenic defects will only in exceptional cases take the trouble.

In affective psychoses the proportion of patients seen personally is considerably smaller than among the improved and recovered schizophrenics. The main reason for this is that schizophrenics, after discharge from the hospital, have, to a great extent, migrated to Oslo and its suburbs, while many with affective psychoses have remained in their homes outside the geographical area chosen for personal re-examination.

The questionnaire method has been used primarily for those with affective psychoses who have good insight into their psychotic periods. In the cases of sixteen persons followed up by questionnaires we have additional information from public health officers. There were essentially no discrepancies between what the doctors and the patients reported. Nineteen patients with reactive psychoses and eight patients with manic-depressive psychoses did not personally answer the questionnaires. In these cases information was obtained from public health officers.

Altogether 130 patients could not be followed up at all, or, in any case, not for a five year period. In these cases we considered the clinical outcome as so uncertain that we could not group them according to clinical outcome. All cases diagnosed as schizophrenia or reactive psychoses with schizophrenic symptoms were included in the schizophrenic group, and the affective groups consisted of the reactive psychoses without schizophrenic symptoms and those diagnosed as manic-depressive psychoses. This classification was valid for the comparison of mortality rates in the three diagnostic groups, which is analyzed in Chapter III.

Table 2 surveys the cases not followed up for five years or more, most of which were deceased (see Table 2).

The foreigners who had left Norway could have been ex-

TABLE 2

Clinical Diagnosis	Deceased After Less than 5 Years	Foreigners who Have Left Norway	Norwegians Migrated to Other Countries	Case Histories Inadequate	Traced, But no Information About Course of Illness	Not Traced After Discharge From Hospital	Total
Schizophrenia	32	6	3	13	3	0	57
Reactive psychoses	27	18	2	0	0	2	49
Manic-depressive psychoses	20	1	2	0	1	0	24
Total not followed up 5 years or more	79	25	7	13	4	2	130

cluded beforehand, as there was little possibility of tracing them. Most of them were admitted to the hospital during the war or shortly afterwards. It would be justifiable to exclude those with inadequate case histories. They were all chronic schizophrenics who were admitted to Gaustad Hospital after the German evacuation of northern Norway. As they were too demented to describe adequately their previous life, and, as no relatives were known, the case histories could not be used for evaluating the correlations between clinical symptoms in the acute stage and the outcome of the illness.

Another lost group were the Norwegian born who had migrated to other countries. For such migrants questionnaires and interviews with relatives and other connections were possible. There remained some cases where no information of the mental state could be obtained.

In four traced patients the course of illness could not be estimated. One of them was seen at home, but point-blank refused a re-examination. In three cases questionnaires concerning patients living in northern and western Norway were answered neither by patients nor public health officers.

A proof of the accuracy of the Norwegian population registration is that only two patients have completely disappeared during our search for them. Having in mind an average observation period of 12.3 years, authors in other countries report considerably more lost patients. According to *Levitt* 59 per cent of closed clinical cases were not expected to be traced in a follow-up twelve years afterwards in the United States (102). This supports our assumption that Norway (like other Scandinavian countries) offers good opportunities for long-term follow-up studies.

Chapter II

CLINICAL PROGNOSIS

1. THE FIVE MAJOR CLINICAL PROGNOSTIC GROUPS

The diagnosis of schizophrenia varies very much according to the definition. This is clearly seen from the last International congress in Zurich as well as from the last survey of schizophrenia by *Bellak* (15).

We face the principal difficulty that there is no general agreement upon the etiology and pathogenesis of schizophrenia. *Bellak* has proposed a multifactorial pathogenesis with the main emphasis on psychodynamic factors. We are skeptical about his stressing the importance of disturbances of ego functions. The psychoanalytic concept of the ego is in principle too subjective to give a reliable basis for diagnostic classification.

The original criterion of *Kraepelin* for dementia praecox was the termination in typical schizophrenic dementia, but *Kraepelin* himself already found recoveries (87).

From a practical point of view it is important to diagnose schizophrenia from the actual clinical picture, without waiting for the long-term outcome. The diagnostic criteria of *Bleuler* are based on this approach (19). In clinical practice some prefer to place stress on a great probability of schizophrenic deterioration, while others emphasize more the presence of the primary symptoms of *Bleuler*, even if the outcome is expected to be favorable. This dualism in diagnostic practice is probably more important for diagnostic controversies than actual disagreement among experienced clinicians on symptomatology and chances of recovery in the individual patient.

Langfeldt has pointedly discussed the need for distinguishing between prognostically unfavorable process schizophrenias and prognostically favorable schizophreniform psychoses (39, 94, 95,

9

96, 97, 98). Whereas the primary symptoms of Bleuler are rather vaguely defined, the process symptoms of *Langfeldt* are as a rule so clear-cut that they can be established when present. In our previous publication we could show, like *Langfeldt*, that when process symptoms are not present, the risk of a schizophrenic deterioration is very small (8). One could, therefore, agree with *Langfeldt* that psychoses without process symptoms should not be diagnosed as schizophrenia. When process symptoms were present, there was always a considerable risk of schizophrenic deterioration. If the term schizophrenia should imply a reasonable prediction about unfavorable outcome, the diagnostic classification should be limited to cases which present process symptoms in the acute stage.

Langfeldt's claim about the poor prognosis could not be confirmed in all cases with process symptoms. In the schizophrenic group we have classified patients who present the process symptoms of *Langfeldt*, as well as some other symptoms which we considered as typical of schizophrenia. In the acute functional psychoses these symptoms proved to be strongly associated with a schizophrenic course of illness.

The typical schizophrenic symptoms, which we previously defined more precisely, are the following (68): 1) Catatonic traits. 2) Emotional blunting. 3) Certain types of depersonalization. 4) Passivity. 5) Disturbances of symbolization in the thought processes. 6) Haptic hallucinations. 7) Special forms of auditory hallucinations, such as the hearing of thoughts, conversation with voices, voices with comments on the patient's movements, and voices coming from the patient's own head or body. 8) Religious and corresponding non-religious megalomania (includes delusions of being Christ, king etc.). 9) Ideas of high descent. 10) Fantasy lover. 11) Fantastic ideas of jealousy. These symptoms we regard as mental automatisms, which, according to conditional reflex experiments, depend more upon general disturbances of the higher nervous activity than upon psychodynamic factors (9, 30, 40, 41, 151).

In order to define schizophrenic deterioration precisely, we have coded patients as deteriorated schizophrenics only when at re-examination they presented the characteristics of one of the various types of defect schizophrenia described by *Leonhard* (101). There were altogether 416 such cases, which made up our *deteriorated schizophrenic* group (see Table 1).

Our second schizophrenic group consisted of improved cases. In this group there are classified patients with minor personality changes reminding of the chronic schizophrenics, but not frankly psychotic. There were 117 such cases.

The third schizophrenic group is composed of 131 patients who have recovered without showing any signs of schizophrenic personality changes. In thirty-nine of the patients there was some reduction of social adaptation, mainly due to mental instability, but also due to neurotic or psychopathic traits.

In the study of acute *affective* psychoses we could distinguish between one group of *reactive* and one group of manic-depressive psychoses (8).

The manic-depressive psychoses have clinical characteristics as defined by *Kraepelin* (87). According to conditional reflex experiments, the symptoms are more related to disturbances of the functions in deeper-lying subcortical structures than to psychodynamic factors (9, 59, 77, 150). Characteristic of these psychoses is an instability of mood. In the acute series this instability was so marked in thirty-four cases that they could only be considered as improved or chronic, whereas forty-nine were classified as recovered. In the total material of 102 manic-depressive cases, fifty-five recovered and forty-seven improved or remained chronic. This shows that those with more insidiously developing manic-depressive psychoses tend to be seriously handicapped by their disease (see Table 14).

The fifth group consisted of so-called reactive psychoses. Clinically this group lacked typical schizophrenic or manic-depressive symptomatology. The clinical picture is that of depression, confusion or paranoid states, and often combinations of such reactions. Predominantly the reactive psychoses occur in persons with neurotic or psychopathic traits. According to psychopathological analysis and conditional reflex experiments, the reactive psychoses very much resemble the neuroses (9). Psychogenic factors play a great role in the causation, but are often combined with somatic stress. The patients regularly recover after a short time from their psychoses. They often relapse, however, and social adaptation tends to be hampered by neurotic conditions. In the acute series seventy-two could only be considered as improved and fifty-eight as recovered (45% recovered). For the total material there were eighty-two recovered and 124 improved (40% recovered). The prognostic outlook is slightly lowered by including the insidiously developing reactive psychoses.

In the following chapters we will compare the three schizophrenic and the two affective groups with respect to various clinical, social and hereditary factors. The next section of this chapter will deal with the characteristics of the various subgroups with schizophrenic and non-schizophrenic courses of illness.

2. CLINICAL SUBGROUPING OF FUNCTIONAL PSYCHOSES

In Chapter IV we have made comparisons between large groups of schizophrenic, reactive and manic-depressive psychoses with regard to several clinical factors. From such comparisons it appears that the various types of functional psychoses cannot be distinctly delimited from each other in the acute stages. Diagnostic predictions as to the course of illness in insidiously developing psychoses are more correctly made than those of acute cases. This is probably because the course of illness has already been taken into consideration to a great extent on admission.

Findings may well be interpreted as supporting a theory of the unitary nature of functional psychoses, with several types of combinations of clinical traits and transitory conditions between three main groups of schizophrenic, reactive and manic-depressive psychoses. For a great number of individual patients it is impossible to predict the outcome. The statistical comparisons between larger groups show such marked differences that we find it justified to consider them in practice as clinical entities.

Within our three clinical entities there are several clinical subgroups. Our experience is that a better knowledge of such subgroups may be even more useful than the major groups for prediction of outcome in the individual case.

Confusingly many clinical subgroups have been described in the literature. It was not wished to add to this confusion by introducing new types. We have tried to separate such groups which are frequently met with and which have previously been well described.

3. THE TYPES OF SCHIZOPHRENIC DEFECTS (DETERIORATED AND IMPROVED)

Patients with a schizophrenic course of illness in our study of acute schizophrenia and schizophreniform psychoses were classified on the basis of the studies of *Leonhard* from 1936 (68, 100). Here the total material is re-classified according to *Leonhard's* monograph of 1959 (101). A few modifications have been made. The most important was that we considered the combined forms of *Leonhard* intermediate forms between the "typical groups," and included them in the groups which they resembled most.

Astrup, in a monograph on conditional reflex studies of schizophrenia, has analyzed material of 306 chronic and 178 acute and subacute schizophrenias. In this study the clinical as well as the experimental characteristics of the schizophrenic subgroups are described in great detail (9). For further descriptions of clinical symptoms illustrated by case histories reference may be made to *Leonhard* and a joint study of *Fish* and *Astrup* on chronic schizophrenics (51, 101). In the following table we present a survey of the schizophrenic subgroups in our total follow-up material (see Table 3).

Affect-laden paraphrenia, schizophasia, and periodic catatonia *Leonhard* designated non-systematic, and the other defects he called systematic schizophrenias. The non-systematic schizophrenias represent to a great extent a transitory group between manic-depressive psychoses and the dementia praecox of *Kraepelin* or the nuclear processes of *Langfeldt* and correspond to the medium forms of *Ey* (46, 87, 94, 98). As analyzed in more detail by *Astrup* in another publication, schizophasia, affect-laden, phonemic and hypochondriacal paraphrenias, autistic and eccentric hebephrenias and, to a great extent, periodic catatonias will mostly appear as slightly deteriorated. All other groups of chronic schizophrenia by and and large showed the characteristics of severe deterioration (9).

Our experience is that when characteristic traits of the

TABLE 3

SURVEY OF SCHIZOPHRENIC SUB-GROUPS

Outcome	Affect - Laden Paraphrenia	Schizophasia	Phonemic Paraphrenia	Hypochondriacal Paraphrenia	Confabulatory Paraphrenia	Expansive Paraphrenia	Fantastic Paraphrenia	Incoherent Paraphrenia	Autistic Hebephrenia	Eccentric Hebephrenia	Shallow Hebephrenia	Silly Hebephrenia	Periodic Catatonia	Parakinetic Catatonia	Speech - Prompt Catatonia	Proskinetic Catatonia	Speech - Inactive Catatonia	Manneristic Catatonia	Negativistic Catatonia	Total
Deteriorated schizophrenics	80	29	37	33	5	12	29	9	15	38	30	17	28	9	9	6	14	8	8	416
Improved schizophrenics	43	13	3	1	0	0	0	0	10	14	0	0	33	0	0	0	0	0	0	117
Total	123	42	40	34	5	12	29	9	25	52	30	17	61	9	9	6	14	8	8	533

systematic schizophrenias can be found, a chronic course can soon after admission be predicted with a great probability. Possibly this means that when such symptoms are found, a chronic course of illness has already set in. At very early stages of schizophrenic psychoses there are, as a rule, less differentiated clinical pictures. These reaction types are the symptom complexes of desultoriness (*"Sprunghaftigkeit"*), thought withdrawal (*"Gedankenentzug"*), and drivelling (*"Faseln"*), described by Carl *Schneider* (4, 52, 153). Clinical and experimental characteristics of these symptom complexes have been described in detail by *Astrup* (9).

The present material confirms the conclusions of *Schneider* and *Astrup* that the symptom complex of thought withdrawal is often reversible. When a chronic course of illness is taken, there develop predominantly slight paranoid defects. Often the symptom complex of thought withdrawal is transferred into the symptom complex of drivelling. The latter symptom complex has a great tendency to chronicity, but, like the former, gives predominantly slight paranoid defects.

The symptom complex of desultoriness has as exemplified in the periodic catatonias, a considerable reversibility. Yet this symptom complex is regularly found in the acute stages of the most severely deteriorated schizophrenics.

As seen from the table the improved schizophrenics predominantly belong to the non-systematic schizophrenias with eighty-nine such cases of 117. This shows clearly that the non-systematic schizophrenias are considerably more reversible than the systematic schizophrenias.

Among the deteriorated cases 156 had severe and 260 slight deterioration. Out of seventy-five personally re-examined chronic schizophrenics living in their homes only five had severe defects. The majority were non-systematic schizophrenias. This illustrates that the possibility of living at home is very small for those with a severe deterioration. Sixty-three of the 118 seen personally in Gaustad Hospital were severely deteriorated, and most were systematic schizophrenias. As illustrations we present a case history of each schizophrenic subgroup.

Affect-laden Paraphrenia This group is characterized by the strong affective anchoring of the delusions. Paranoia-resembling paraphrenic cases clearly satisfy the criteria. At the acute stages the clinical pictures are often so uncharacteristic that non-schizophrenic disorders were originally diagnosed. Clinically the psychoses usually start with the symptom complex of drivelling. The affect-laden paraphrenics very often have social remissions and even some recoveries (see page 32). Our cases correspond to some of the paranoias and systematic paraphrenias of *Kraepelin* (87).

No. 14762. Male, born 1886. His father and a sister were allegedly schizophrenic, but case histories were not available. One brother had inventory paranoia and another brother was markedly schizoid.

The patient had a self-assertive prepsychotic personality. At the age of forty-nine, after the death of his wife, he chose a female doctor as a fantasy lover. As he was annoying the doctor very much, he was admitted to Gaustad Hospital in 1938. He was discharged after several years' stay in the hospital, but continued to trouble his fantasy lover and was re-admitted to the hospital in 1954. During all the years since his first admission, he had been practically unchanged. He was sincerely convinced that the doctor loved him; and that an underground nazist cabal consisting of doctors and several prominent persons did not, however, allow her to express her real feelings toward him. Once he had seen Christ, and another time he had had auditory pseudohallucinations. The patient had since his youth worked at inventions, and believed that he had solved an important aero-dynamic problem.

When speaking about his fantasy lover and the persecutions the patient showed very great emotional reactions. This was correlated by violent respiratory and plethysmographic reactions in experiments. The general disturbances of the higher nervous activity were slight.

Schizophasia The main characteristics are the severe disturbances of speech combined with a well-ordered behavior. Delusions and hallucinations are as a rule absent. There are often remissions in the course of the illness. *Leonhard's* concept of schizophasia is wider than that of *Kraepelin* (87, 101).

No. 50. Female, born 1914. A half-sister was treated for a manic-depressive psychosis.

The prepsychotic personality was rather harmonious. At the age of thirty-four the patient became psychotic, and she was admitted to Gaustad Hospital in 1950. At admission she was elated, presented flight of ideas and also, periodically, incoherence. She revealed depersonalization and disturbances of symbolization. In addition she had megalomanic ideas, ideas of high descent and a fantasy lover. Auditory and haptic hallucinations were established.

During the hospital stay the clinical picture gradually became dominated by severe paraphasic disturbances of speech. The patient spoke very much, and, although every sentence was understandable, the logical connection between her utterances could only be guessed at. She often used words incorrectly and was especially inclined to mix up abstract and concrete meanings. Delusions and hallucinations seemed periodically to be present, but the patient could not adequately relate on such experiences because of the disturbances of speech. At work the patient was quite clever, and her behavior was orderly. Emotionally the patient was mostly euphoric, showing some swingings of mood combined with psychomotor excitation.

In conditional reflex experiments the disturbances of the higher nervous activity were slight.

Phonemic Paraphrenia In the chronic state the verbal hallucinosis is the main psychotic trait. Often the voices are heard within the head and make comments on the patient's thoughts. The content tends to be bound up with personal feelings and experiences. This type corresponds to some of the chronic deliriums with hallucinations described by French authors, or the dementia paranoides mitis of *Kraepelin* (87).

No. 17112. Female, born 1906. No close relatives were psychotic.

The patient had a sensitive prepsychotic personality with sthenic traits. She became psychotic at the age of 42 and was admitted to Gaustad Hospital in 1949. The initial symptoms were

ideas of reference and suspiciousness. At admission she presented
disturbances of symbolization, felt hypnotized and said she was
used as a medium. She heard voices coming from without, as
well as from her own head.

In 1959 the patient was re-examined in her home. Now she
only heard voices talking within her head. The voices repeated
what she thought, and said very unpleasant things. Especially they
accused her of having a low sexual morality, which she considered
not true. The patient had learned not to care so much about her
voices, and the mood was slightly euphoric.

Conditional reflex experiments showed in 1957 slight disturbances of the higher nervous activity.

Hypochondriacal Paraphrenia   Central symptoms in this
group are combinations of auditory hallucinations and hypochondriacal sensations. Their hallucinations are usually more
elementary and less bound up with personal experiences and feelings than in the phonemic paraphrenia. Decisive for the differential diagnosis is the presence of haptic hallucinations, which are
absent in phonemic paraphrenia. The hypochondriacal paraphrenia, like the previously mentioned subgroup, corresponds to
the chronic deliriums with hallucinations as described by French
authors and the dementia paranoides mitis of *Kraepelin* (87).

No. 16798. Male, born 1903. His father and his brother suffered from hypochondriacal paraphrenia.

The patient had a self-assertive prepsychotic personality. He
fell ill at the age of thirty-eight and was admitted to Gaustad Hospital in 1948. At admission he revealed depersonalization, feelings
of passivity and disturbances of symbolization. He also had megalomanic, hypochondriacal and persecutory delusions. Furthermore he believed that his food was poisoned, causing changes in
his genital organs.

At the period of re-examination bizarre, hypochondriacal
ideas were most outstanding in the clinical picture. He thought
that his nose was rotten, so that small pieces were falling out and
that hundreds of worms were running out of his stomach. He also
heard voices shouting into his ears, but the voices had no such
distressing content as in the case of phonemic paraphrenia. In

speech and behavior the patient was orderly, and he was clever at work. A permanently morose and dissatisfied mood was characteristic.

In conditional reflex experiments the disturbances of the higher nervous activity were slight.

Confabulatory Paraphrenia These patients tell unbelievable stories about personal experiences. The confabulations generally have a fantastic quality and are concerned with other parts of the world, other worlds, or even the moon and stars. As a rule expansive traits are present. This subgroup is one of the paraphrenias described by *Kraepelin* (87), but *Leonhard* has defined the entity more precisely (101).

No. 15638. Male, born 1922. His father was rather schizoid, and his mother suffered from expansive paraphrenia.

The patient had a schizoid prepsychotic personality. He became psychotic at the age of twenty-one and was admitted to Gaustad Hospital in 1943. At admission he revealed depersonalization and feelings of passivity. He believed that he was Christ and had imperative auditory hallucinations.

At re-examination expansively colored delusions dominated the clinical picture. His delusions changed from time to time. He could relate that he had been in America, France, Poland, and Russia, and also give a wealth of details about these imaginary travels. He had even been on the moon, where the soil was cultivated in quite another way than on earth. Futhermore he told how he lived in the Stone Age and pulled great stones with a rope. This patient had a markedly euphoric mood. In behavior he was less orderly than the previously reported slightly deteriorated cases, and he was less efficient at work.

According to conditional reflex experiments he revealed rather great disturbances of the higher nervous activity.

Expansive Paraphrenia Expansive behavior and expansive ideas dominate the clinical picture. The patients adapt a kind of haughty pose and take on a superior attitude when dealing with others. This distinguishes them from the fantastic and confabulatory paraphrenias, where the grandiose delusions do not lead to expansive behavior. *Kraepelin's* expansive paraphrenia is less circumscribed than the group of *Leonhard* (87, 101).

No. 64. Male, born 1909. There was no information about psychoses in his immediate family.

Before psychosis the patient was a psychopath with hysteric character traits. He became ill at the age of thirty-five and was admitted to Gaustad Hospital in 1950. In the initial clinical picture he presented depersonalization, feelings of passivity and disturbances of symbolization. Futhermore, he had hypochondriacal, persecutory and megalomanic delusions, auditory, gustatory and haptic hallucinations.

At re-examination the clinical picture was dominated by expansive delusions and behavior. The patient was convinced that he was the cleverest thinker in the world and ought to lead the hospital as well as the political activities of the society. He used high-sounding phrases and continually produced secret documents, which were written in code. This patient was rather euphoric and less orderly in speech and behavior than the slight paranoid defects.

In conditional reflex experiments he revealed great general disturbances of the higher nervous activity.

Fantastic Paraphrenia   A great number of characteristic clinical phenomena tend to be combined in this subgroup, such as: 1) Expansive delusions. 2) Somatic sensations, often of a grotesque and fantastic character. 3) Mass phenomena (visions of thousands of people being tortured and crying.). 4) Misidentification of persons. 5) Fantastic confabulations *a*) The borders between life and death vanish. *b*) Age and time lose their proportions. *c*) Nature seems alive like human beings.

Only in a minority of the fantastic paraphrenias are all the mentioned symptoms present. These psychoses correspond roughly to the fantastic paraphrenias and some of the systematic paraphrenias of *Kraepelin*. Many cases in the three last mentioned groups have the characteristics of the chronic deliriums with systematic evolution described by French authors (87).

No. 14823. Male, born 1905. There was no information about psychoses in his family.

The patient had a schizoid prepsychotic personality. He became psychotic at the age of thirty-three and was admitted to Gaustad Hospital in 1939. At admission he revealed feelings of passivity, auditory hallucinations and persecutory delusions.

During the period of re-examination the patient presented several traits characteristic of fantastic paraphrenia. He related scenes of horrible torture and mass murders in which all the people in the town were killed; and that he also had been killed himself several times and had seen his soul leaving his body. He stated that there was a lion in his body, and in his head a weight of 100,000 tons. He also misidentified strangers, declaring that he had met them previously. Like the confabulatory paraphrenias he could relate about imaginary travels to other countries. Furthermore, he had megalomanic ideas and thought he was very rich. In his moods the patient varied between euphoria and anger. He had to be in a closed ward, but was quite clever at work.

In conditional reflex experiments the disturbances of the higher nervous activity were great.

Incoherent Paraphrenia This subgroup is characterized by a severe dissociation of speech, which makes an ordered conversation impossible, and, in contrast to the schizophasias, their general behavior is also disordered. These patients are absorbed by hallucinatory experiences and have no interest in what goes on around them. They tend towards severe deterioration, and correspond to the dementia paranoides gravis of *Kraepelin* or the *"schizokare Verblödung"* of *Mauz* (87, 111).

No. 15070. Male, born 1912. No psychoses in his immediate family were known.

Before psychosis the patient had a self-assertive personality. He became psychotic at the age of twenty-five and was admitted to Gaustad Hospital in 1941. The onset of illness was rather insidious, with changes of personality, impulsivity and tantrums preceding the manifest psychotic symptoms. At admission he presented a mixed paranoid-hebephrenic state with marked emotional blunting, persecutory delusions, feelings of passivity, depersonalization, and auditory and haptic hallucinations.

At re-examination this patient presented the continuous auditory hallucinations, characteristic of incoherent paraphrenia. He talked loudly to the voices, and it was not possible to converse with him. To questions he answered with incoherent speech. Clinically this patient was considered more deteriorated than the previously reported paranoid cases. In conditional reflex experiments he also showed more severe disturbances of the higher nervous activity.

Autistic Hebephrenia A combination of emotional blunting and extreme autism is characteristic of this group. The patients shut themselves up actively, avoid contact with others and tend to reject attempts of others to communicate with them. This subgroup has only been differentiated by *Kleist* and *Leonhard* (82, 101). Autism is common in schizophrenics. An active seclusion unrelated to delusions, hallucinations or catatonic symptoms is found only in the autistic hebephrenias.

No. 16443. Male, born 1907. His father was nervous. A brother had had a period of marked jealousy but he did not receive psychiatric treatment.

The patient had a sensitive prepsychotic personality. He fell ill at the age of forty and was admitted to Gaustad Hospital in 1947. The initial symptoms were ideas of reference and suspiciousness. At admission he had fantastic ideas of jealousy and hypochondriacal and persecutory delusions. He also presented feelings of passivity, depersonalization, disturbances of symbolization, and gustatory and haptic hallucinations.

At re-examination no hallucinations or delusions could be established, but he had a marked emotional blunting and was extremely autistic. He never associated with other patients, and his facial expression was stiff and impenetrable. His mood apparently was discontented and slightly irritable. At work the patient was quite clever, and conditional reflex experiments revealed only slight disturbances of the higher nervous activity.

Eccentric Hebephrenia. Affective blunting is a central symptom in this subgroup. The patients also regularly have mannerisms and eccentric behavior. There is something cheerless about their mood. They may tend to be depressed, but more often are irritable and aggressive. *Kraepelin* has described a depressive type of dementia praecox, which has several of the characteristics of eccentric hebephrenia (87).

No. 15839. Female, born 1909. An aunt suffered from reactive psychosis, an uncle from schizophasia and another uncle was reportedly insane.

The patient had a schizoid prepsychotic personality. She experienced an unhappy marriage, during which she became psychotic at the age of thiry-three. The initial symptoms were depression, impulsivity and tantrums. In 1944 the patient was admitted to Gaustad Hospital. At admission she presented psychomotor excitation and mannerisms. The affect was rather eccentric, but there was no marked emotional blunting. Also, incoherence and auditory hallucinations were noticed.

When re-examined, she denied hallucinations and did not appear hallucinated. No delusions could be established. She appeared rather cheerless and depressed, but the main impression was one of a severe affective flattening. Often she could be angry and irritable, and sometimes hypochondriacal. Her behavior was rather monotonous with repeated complaints and demands. Otherwise she was well-ordered in behavior and speech and could work quite well in the hospital.

In experiments the disturbances of the higher nervous activity were slight.

Shallow Hebephrenia   This group is mainly distinguished by an affective blunting. The affective flattening passes beyond a defect in interests and leads to a deficiency in initiative. The mood is mainly characterized by euphoria or indifferent satisfaction. From time to time the patients hallucinate, and then become excited and aggressive. This group corresponds to the dementia simplex of *Kraeplin* and *Bleuler* (19, 87).

No. 16410. Female, born 1924. The father was insane, but the clinical picture could not be ascertained.

Before her illness the patient had a harmonious personality. She became psychotic at the age of twenty-one and was admitted to Gaustad Hospital in 1946. The initial symptoms were changes of personality, impulsivity and tantrums. At admission the patient revealed marked emotional blunting. She had auditory and haptic hallucinations, talked incoherently, had feelings of passivity, depersonalization and megalomanic delusions.

At re-examination the flattening of affect was verp pronounced. She said that she was in good spirits, and her mood state was one of indifferent satisfaction. During later years she often heard voices. In the hallucinated periods she might become very excited and aggressive, but with chlorpromazine she became quieter. Some mannerisms which were more characteristic of eccentric than shallow hebephrenia were also observed. The patient could carry on an ordered conversation, but, because of lack of initiative, her work capacity was small.

In conditional reflex experiments there were considerable disturbances of the higher nervous activity with marked signs of dissociation.

Silly Hebephrenia . In this group an intensive affective blunting is associated with a mood which varies from content to mild cheerfulness. A smile or even a giggle is particularly characteristic, and this becomes prominent under the influence of every external stimulus. The silly *"läppische"* hebephrenias seem to be a well circumscribed defect state; described by *Kraepelin* and his predecessors and taken over practically unchanged by *Leonhard* (87, 101).

No. 16124. Male, born 1923. Only remote relatives were known to be insane.

The premorbid personality was harmonious. He became psychotic at the age of twenty-two and was admitted to Gaustad Hospital in 1945. The initial symptoms were ideas of reference. At admission the patient presented psychomotor blocking, incoherence and feelings of passivity. He had also auditory hallucinations. The dominant clinical symptom was a marked emotional blunting.

In this patient the schizophrenic process progressed very rapidly, and at re-examination he presented an intensive affective blunting, which was associated with a contented and mildly cheerful mood. Characteristic of silly hebephrenias, he smiled and giggled, — in particular, when spoken to. Periodically he hallucinated, but did not bother about the hallucinations, and even denied them. He was completely unable to work, and could only loiter around in a happy-go-lucky way.

In conditional reflex experiments there were great disturbances of the higher nervous activity with marked signs of dissociation.

Periodic Catatonia Clinically these psychoses have hyper-kinetic and akinetic phases. Remissions occur regularly, and the deterioration may vary much in degree. If the defects are mild, they show themselves in a general psychic lameness. In the most severe defects the patients have a dullness which is reminiscent of an organic deterioration. On the basis of the acute symptoms it was not possible for us to predict which cases would recover or which would deteriorate. In the next section of this chapter the recovered cases will be dealt with (see page 38). That catatonic schizophrenia may run a periodic course is well known. The separation of periodic catatonia as a subgroup is mainly based on the follow-up studies of *Kleist, Leonhard* and their colleagues (101).

> No. 16982. Male, born 1915. The grandfather, two uncles of the mother, an aunt of the father, three cousins and three siblings were insane. Case histories were available for the three siblings, all of whom had periodic catatonia.
>
> The patient had a harmonious premorbid personality. At the age of twenty-five he had his first psychotic attack, precipitated by war events. This was apparently a catatonic excitement, which passed over without hospitalization. In the following years he had several periods of insomnia and excitement, and in 1949 he was admitted to Gaustad Hospital.
>
> At admission he was mute, blocked, and presented a typical catatonia. After convulsive treatment he improved and could tell that he had auditory and visual hallucinations, ideas of refer-ence and persecutory delusions. His condition varied between periods of psychomotor inhibition and excitation.
>
> When re-examined the patient had a psychic lameness with an impoverishment of drive, but also impulsive excitements. He was quite clever at work. After a leucotomy in 1956, he could be discharged to his home and do farm work.
>
> In conditional reflex experiments the disturbances of the higher nervous activity were not so great as in the systematic catatonias.

Parakinetic Catatonia The central symptoms are the para-kinesias, which can be rich in variety. Actions are carried out in an unnatural, awkward way, and the movements take place jerkily, so that they are reminiscent of choreiform movements.

This subgroup corresponds to the manneristic catatonia of *Kraepelin* (87).

Common for all the systematic catatonias is that they represent disturbances of rather circumscript psychomotor functions, and in this way are closely analogous to neurological diseases. The precise delimitation of these forms has mainly been attempted by those who follow the principles of *Kleist* and *Leonhard* (82, 101).

> No. 15771. Male, born 1916. The father and a sister were probably psychotic, but not treated in hospitals. A brother suffered from parakinetic catatonia.
>
> The premorbid personality appeared to be hysteric with some traits of antisocial behavior. He became psychotic at the age of twenty-two, kept to his bed during the day, was strongly inhibited and spoke incomprehensibly. In 1944 the patient was admitted to Gaustad Hospital. He presented a typical catatonic picture with echolalia, echopraxia, blocking, grimaces, and mannerisms. His speech was incoherent, and he had auditory hallucinations. Affectively he revealed emotional blunting as well as perplexity.
>
> At the time of re-examination the patient had hallucinatory periods and shouted to the voices. He kept good contacts with his home and showed interest in his surroundings. It was especially characteristic that he grimaced a good deal and carried out his movements in an unnatural awkward way. He used to jump about stereotypically and said this was in order to straighten himself up. He spoke in short, sharp utterances, and the words sounded choppy. The patient did not belong to the most deteriorated systematic catatonias, but had only small working ability.
>
> In conditional reflex experiments the disturbances of the higher nervous activity were less pronounced than in the majority of the systematic catatonic defects.

Speech-prompt Catatonia "Talking beside the point" (*"Vorbeireden"*) is the most essential symptom of this type of catatonic defect. The patients frequently give the correct answer to the simplest indifferent questions. The more difficult and emotionally charged the questions become, the more regularly will the patients disregard the point. The facial expression is peculiarly vacuous.

No. 82. Male, born 1919. The father and an aunt were considered as nervous, but not treated in hospitals. A sister and a brother were psychotic, and both suffered from speech-prompt catatonia.

Before his illness the patient had a harmonious personality. At the age of twenty-eight he suddenly experienced a panic feeling and afterwards turned seclusive and took less interest in work. He was admitted to Gaustad Hospital in 1950 because of impulsive behavior and excitement. In the hospital he presented a catatonic picture with variations from blocking to excitation, mannerisms and negativism. He spoke incoherently, had feelings of passivity and auditory hallucinations. During the following years he was apathetic, with outbursts of excitement and aggressiveness.

At re-examination the patient did not appear to bother much about his environment. His facial expression was particularly empty and stiff, and the motor activity had an element of constraint about it. In contrast to the strong inhibition of general behavior, there was a promptness to answer questions. Answers could be obtained to every question, even if meaningless, and as a rule he disregarded the point of the question. He was, for example, asked how many stars there were in the sky and promptly replied eleven. The patient could do no work and had to live in a disturbed ward.

In conditional reflex experiments, he presented the most severe types of disturbances of the higher nervous activity.

Proskinetic Catatonia The main characteristic of this defect type is the tendency to turn towards the examiner and allow themselves to be directed automatically. When questioned, the patients regularly begin to murmur unintelligibly.

No. 16155. Female, born 1922. A brother suffered from periodic catatonia. Another brother and an aunt had proskinetic catatonias as did the patient.

About the premorbid personality there was incomplete information. The patient became psychotic at the age of eighteen with sudden excitement. In the following years she was periodically excited and incoherent with impulsivity and tantrums. She was admitted to Gaustad Hospital in 1945.

At admission the psychomotor symptoms varied between blocking and excitation. She had no hallucinations or delusions, but marked emotional blunting.

When re-examined that patient was not able to carry on a conversation, but murmured unintelligibly. Very characteristic was a tendency to turn towards the examiner. When the examiner presented his hand, she always took it, even if she was told not to do it. If one pressed lightly on any part of her body, then she would move in the direction of the pressure, and any position determined by the examiner would be taken up. She apparently had a marked affective flattening with an unconcerned sort of self-satisfaction, lived in a disturbed ward, and could not work. This patient was not studied with conditional reflex experiments.

Speech-inactive Catatonia . These patients give answers slowly and in the later stages generally not at all. During the examination one can regularly see that they are whispering, sometimes laughing, and at other times looking irritated. They are seemingly always occupied by hallucinations. From time to time they can become markedly excited, scream and shout. Some of the negativistic forms of *Kraepelin* present the characteristic shift between speech inhibition and excitation (87).

No. 15773. Female, born in 1915. The mother suffered from eccentric hebephrenia, and an aunt was considered as very nervous, but not treated in a psychiatric hospital.

The patient had a harmonious premorbid personality. She became psychotic at the age of twenty and was admitted to Gaustad Hospital in 1944. The initial symptoms were mainly changes of personality. At admission the patient had no marked catatonic symptoms, apart from some psychomotor blocking. She spoke incoherently, was emotionally blunted, and presented depersonalization, auditory, gustatory, haptic, and visual hallucinations. No delusions could be established.

During the hospital stay the patient developed a severe deterioration. At the time of re-examination she had periods of catatonic excitation. She was very inhibited, slow in movements and mutistic. During examination it could be observed that she was whispering, sometimes laughing and at other times looking irritated. She appeared completely uninterested in the examiner, looked away and seemed to be occupied by hallucinations. The patient had to be in a disturbed ward and needed care in all ways with eating, dressing, and cleanliness.

In conditional reflex experiments she presented the most severe types of disturbances of the higher nervous activity.

Manneristic Catatonia   In this type an increasing impoverishment of involuntary motor activity occurs, resulting in a stiffness of posture and movements. In addition there are mannerisms, which in the beginning are more prominent than the stiffness. As the illness develops, motor activity is restricted more and more to a few stereotypically repeated movements. *Leonhard* has pointed out that the psychomotor disturbances had some resemblances to Parkinsonism (101).

No. 16317. Male, born 1914. There was no information about psychoses in the near family.

Before his illness, the patient had a harmonious personality. The disease started at the age of twenty-eight with catatonic excitation, and in 1946 the patient was admitted to Gaustad Hospital. He was then blocked, apathetic with lack of initiative, spoke incoherently, and told of persecutory delusions and auditory hallucinations.

During the hospital stay he developed a severe deterioration. In the beginning he showed some mannerisms, collected worthless things, and had a tendency to self-mutilation and to destroy things. But gradually an impoverishment of movement occurred. This resulted in a stiffness of posture and movements with a stiff facial expression. During the last years the patient has been mutistic. He did not appear hallucinated and had no excited periods, but he could not work and he lived in a ward with much nursing supervision.

In conditional reflex experiments the disturbances of the higher nervous activity were very great.

Negativistic Catatonia   This type is to a great extent diametrically the opposite of proskinetic catatonia. The negativism in these patients seems to be of a rather automatic nature. Often one can observe an ambitendency which shows that it is more than an irritable rejection and that a true negativism is present. If it is possible to put the patient in a friendly mood, he will carry out some requests, but often only partially. This subgroup corresponds roughly to the negativistic deterioration described by *Kraepelin* (87).

> No. 16827. Male, born 1924. The mother was probably psychotic, but not treated in a psychiatric hospital. His father was eccentric, one brother had epilepsy, and two brothers had been imprisoned for criminal acts.
>
> The patient had a schizoid premorbid personality. He became psychotic at the age of twenty-four and was admitted to Gaustad Hospital in 1948. Some years previously he had had a nervous period, and the initial symptoms of the psychosis were changes of personality in the direction of seclusiveness. He was admitted because of suicidal attempts. In the hospital his condition fluctuated between catatonic excitation and stupor with negativism. Speech was incoherent. Emotionally he presented a combination of depression and emotional blunting.
>
> At re-examination the patient was mutistic and extremely negativistic. Often he could be excited and aggressive, especially if an attempt was made to counteract his negativism. The motor behavior was impulsive, which made him operate awkwardly and jerkily, and caused a peculiar twisting of his head. The patient had no working ability and was in a disturbed ward in the hospital.
>
> Because of his negativism, conditional reflex experiments did not give much information, but pointed to severe disturbances of the higher nervous activity.

For each of the numbered patients referred to, detailed information about the disturbances of the higher nervous activity are shown in tables of another publication by *Astrup* (9).

4. THE TYPES OF PSYCHOSES WITH NON-SCHIZOPHRENIC COURSE OF ILLNESS

In the same way as the presence of symptoms characteristic of various types of schizophrenic deterioration may at an early stage contribute to prediction of a schizophrenic course of illness,

TABLE 4

SURVEY OF PSYCHOSES WITH NON-SCHIZOPHRENIC COURSE OF ILLNESS

Outcome	Affect - Laden Paraphrenia	Anxiety - Ecstasy Psychoses	Sensitive Delusions of Reference	Querulent Paranoia	Persecutory-affective Psychoses	Stupor - Confusion Psychoses	Periodic Catatonia	Motility Psychoses	Confusional - Hysteric Psychoses	Other Hysteric Psychoses	Pseudo - Neurotic Schizophrenia	Pseudo - Psychopathic Schizophrenia	Depersonalization Psychoses	Reactive Depressions	Typical Manic - Depressive Psychoses	Total
Recovered schizophrenics	10	30	10	0	0	20	36	7	0	0	4	0	14	0	0	131
Reactive psychoses	0	0	32	12	21	0	0	3	30	11	22	7	25	43	0	206
Manic-depressive psychoses	1	18	0	0	0	0	0	0	0	0	0	0	16	0	67	102
Total	11	48	42	12	21	20	36	10	30	11	26	7	55	43	67	439

a better knowledge of the types of functional psychoses which recover may help to predict a favorable outcome. In the following table is given a survey of the types of psychoses in which no schizophrenic deterioration developed (see Table 4).

We would stress that our fifteen groups of prognostically favorable functional psychoses are not sharply delimited, either from each other, or from the types with a schizophrenic course of illness. All the recovered schizophrenics have in fact been suspected of schizophrenic deterioration on the strength of the clinical symptomatologies, and could be placed within the wide categories of schizophreniform or schizoaffective psychoses (68).

In the group of *affect-laden paraphrenia* we have eleven cases which in the acute stage were characterized by systematized delusions and the symptom complex of drivelling. Taking into consideration that we have 123 affect-laden paraphrenias with a schizophrenic course of illness, this syndrome has a great tendency to chronicity. This is in good accordance with the experiences of *Leonhard* (101). In *Astrup's* experimental series with short observation periods, not one of forty-three cases with systematized delusions was considered to be recovered (9). It seems that with longer observation periods there may be sligthly better chances of reversibility of such syndromes. All but two of the eleven affect-laden cases were socially well adapted. This type of psychosis is illustrated by a case report.

> No. 16452. Female, born 1898. A brother committed suicide.
>
> The patient had a schizoid premorbid personality. Some years prior to the outbreak, the patient had a nervous period. At the age of forty-seven she started to develop ideas of reference, and she was admitted to Gaustad Hospital in 1947. In the center of the clinical picture were persecutory, systematized delusions with a marked disturbance of symbolization. She felt also hypnotized and believed somebody was writing on her lips. The patient related about visual and auditory hallucinations. She heard voices from the surroundings, as well as from her own head, and believed her enemies would shoot her and her son. After a few days stay in the hospital the patient, at the wish of her husband, was discharged as insane. The hospital diagnosis was paranoid reactive psychosis.
>
> In 1956 the patient was re-examined in her home. She

claimed that she recovered in the course of six months, and the husband confirmed what she said. According to the clinical examination the patient could be considered as completely recovered.

In the second group we have forty-eight patients with *anxiety-ecstasy psychoses*. They appear in two forms, either as ecstatic excitements or a depressions with strong anxiety. Often a patient may have both types of reactions. In contrast to the typical manic-depressive psychoses, they have always paranoid traits in the clinical picture. This type of psychosis is described in detail by *Leonhard,* who points out that they often are erroneously considered to develop schizophrenic defect (52, 101). We have limited the group to cases with clearly schizophrenic symptoms, and in particular to cases with the symptom complex of "thought withdrawal." In the experimental material of *Astrup* such cases had a favorable short-time prognosis, and resembled very much the typical manic-depresive psychoses in experiments (9). In the present material, eighteen belong to the manic-depressive group. Actually the differences between ecstasy and manic elation are rather subtle. In melancholia it is often a subjective evaluation if the dominant emotional disturbance is depression or anxiety. For our total follow-up series in the vast majority of cases with the symptom complex of thought withdrawal, the illness has taken a schizophrenic course. Characteristic of the anxiety-ecstasy psychoses is not only this symptom complex, but strong affective traits, acute onset, and short-lasting schizophrenic symptoms. There was reduced social adaptation in thirteen cases, mainly because of mental instability. A case report follows:

No. 16453. Female, born 1923. No genetic loading of psychoses.

Before psychosis the patient had a sensitive personality. Her mother was operated for cancer mammae and in the autumn of 1946 had a relapse with metastases. The patient was very afraid that her mother should get to know how serious this was. Then she gradually became restless and agitated and was admitted to Gaustad Hospital February 11, 1947.

In the hospital the patient was ecstatic, sexually excited and felt that somebody acted upon her genital organs with electric current. She heard voices, which sometimes came from without and at other times carried on discussions within her head. Her thoughts were directed and came back to her from the walls as an echo. She believed she had solved all the problems of cancer, death and the eternal life. After five months stay in the hospital the patient was discharged as insane, but was soon afterwards admitted to another mental hospital.

She was re-examined in her home in 1956. Since the end of 1947, apart from a minor depression, she had been mentally healthy. The psychotic experiences she remembered in all details, but had complete insight. The patient married in 1952 and lived happily with her husband.

A group of forty-two patients have been classified as having *sensitive delusions of reference* according to the descriptions of *Kretschmer* (90). Only ten of them had schizophrenic symptoms. Considering that 142 of those with schizophrenic defects presented ideas of reference on admission to the hospital (Table 22), one should be careful in predicting a favorable outcome when typical schizophrenic symptoms are present. *Langfeldt* states that ideas of reference are prognostically favorable (95). In the clearly non-schizophrenic reactive group as many as thirty-two have such psychoses, but the majority of them are mixed paranoid-depressive states. The ideas of reference can be considered to a great extent as secondary delusions on the basis of depression, disturbances of consciousness, and sensitive personality structures. In twenty-five cases there was reduced social adaptation, mainly related to neurotic or psychopathic traits. A case history is presented as an illustration.

No. 16027. Female, born 1920. A grandmother was insane and her father was sentenced for murder.

Before psychosis the patient had a markedly sensitive personality. Among factors precipitating the psychosis could be mentioned infidelity of her husband and poor housing conditions. Her disease started with depression, and after three months she was admitted to Gaustad Hospital in 1945. The clinical picture was dominated by delusions of reference. The patient thought that people accused her of treason (it was just after the German occupation), and of having sexual intercourse with her own brother and that through the press and over the radio people were informed about her "crimes." The patient had auditory hallucinations, felt hypnotized and stated that foreign thoughts were coming into her head. After three months stay in the hospital the patient could be discharged as not insane with the diagnosis of schizophrenia.

At discharge the patient appeared rather autistic. When re-examined eleven years afterwards she had recovered completely and lived happily with her husband.

Kolle stresses that paranoia with regard to clinical symptomatology as well as genetic loading is closely related to the schizophrenias. The only exception was *querulent paranoia* (85, 86). It was reasonable to separate twelve of the latter as a subgroup. They are all found in the reactive group and present, as a rule, clear-cut paranoid states. In psychoses with a schizophrenic course of illness only nineteen presented marked ideas of revindication (Table 22). We assume that querulent paranoia and, in general, states with ideas of revindication in the long run should not be expected to turn out as schizophrenias. Ten of the twelve cases had at re-examination similar querulent tendencies as before admission.

No. 15222. Female, born 1897. No psychosis in the near family.

The patient had an outspoken self-assertive premorbid personality. She was divorced and lived together with her two sons. The last years before the outbreak of the psychosis, association with the patient had been very difficult. She became litigious, and falsely charged her eldest son with violence, theft, deception and defalcation, which was not true. Shortly afterwards she set fire to the family's house, which her sons possessed, and after this she was admitted to Gaustad Hospital in 1942 for judicial psychiatric observation. She protested violently against the hospital admission, which she considered as a plot of all those who were against her. During the hospital stay she was in strong opposition and threatened revenge for the "unlawful" detention in the hospital. After five months the patient was discharged as not insane with the diagnosis of reactive psychosis.

In 1957 the patient was re-examined in her home. It appeared that since discharge she had been occupied mainly in writing about the "injustice" she had experienced. She had written to the Department of Justice in order to have the judicial psychiatric certificate set aside. Her opinion was that the whole society was rotten. She complained especially about various psychiatrists, who, she considered, had assisted her family in destroying her life. She had great piles of documents and spoke with great emotion about the "injustice" she had suffered.

As a separate group we have twenty-one patients with *persecutory-affective psychoses*. None of them have schizophrenic symptoms. These cases are phenomenologically rather parallel to the non-schizophrenic sensitive delusions of reference. The persecutory delusions have predominantly the character of exaggerated interpretations of hostile attitudes of persons with whom they associate. Most people from time to time experience a feeling of hostility from other individuals or social groups. On the basis of a depressed state or disturbance of consciousness, hostile feelings may easily be interpreted in a delusional manner. At re-examination seven had reduced social adaptation because of neurotic or psychopathic traits. The following case may serve as an example.

No. 16328. Female, born 1905. A half-sister of the mother suffered from affect-laden paraphrenia.

Before psychosis the patient had a self-assertive personality. She married in 1941, and the marriage was very unhappy. Her husband drank and sometimes accused her of having poisoned his food. In 1944 the patient made an attempt at suicide, because she considered her marriage as intolerable. She left her husband in March 1946, but went back to him six weeks prior to admission in Gaustad Hospital. After returning to her husband she began to fear that he would kill her, and also that others might kill her. In the hospital she was stuporous and negativistic, would not eat, because she believed the food was poisoned. She was very depressed and had auditory hallucinations. After three months stay in the hospital the patient could be discharged as not insane with the diagnosis of reactive psychosis.

In 1957 the patient was re-examined. She set her persecutory experiences in relation to the conflicts with her husband. Now she had divorced her husband, had been working since discharge from the hospital, and was in good mental health.

Leonhard has described an entity of *stupor-confusion psychoses* which should be separated from the schizophrenias, although they very much resemble acute states of schizophasia. These psychoses have as a main trait confusion, combined with psychomotor excitation or inhibition. They often change from excited confusion to stupor. For further details about the clinical characteristics reference is made to the monographs of *Leonhard* and *Fish* (52, 101). We have classified twenty patients in this group. They present mostly paranoid ideas, and often in the form of the symptom complex of thought withdrawal. They resemble very much the anxiety-ecstasy psychoses. Yet their psychomotor symptoms may be very difficult to distinguish from periodic catatonia, motility psychoses or confused hysteric psychoses. They have confusion in common with the hysteric psychoses. We have limited the stupor-confusion psychoses to cases which present some typical schizophrenic symptoms. These psychoses are apparently similar clinical entities as oneirophrenia, confusional schizophrenia, or benign stupors described by other authors (15, 104, 115, 144). It is, however, important to know that such cases have an essentially good prognosis. At re-examination five had reduced social adaptation, mainly due to mental instability. A case history is given for illustration.

No. 2. Male, born 1912. No genetic loading of psychoses was known.

Before psychosis the patient had a neurotic personality structure with sensitive traits. After a quarrel with his landlord and alcoholic abuse he became confused and excited and was admitted to Gaustad Hospital in 1950. He heard voices, with which he argued. Also, he felt an electric current in his head, and thought his body and thoughts were influenced by gas and various colored lamps. The patient acted as if he was an aeroplane, buzzing and moving his arms as if flying. He alternated between psychomotor excitation and stupor. During some days he was mutistic, and would communicate only by means of a sort of symbolic language. Emotionally he revealed depression and perplexity. After 4 months the patient could be discharged as not insane.

When re-examined in his home, he showed a complete recovery from his psychosis, managed his work well and enjoyed a harmonious marriage.

Periodic catatonia has already been mentioned in the schizophrenic group (page 25). These psychoses are characterized by acute onsets and rather violent psychomotor symptoms. Out of ninety-seven cases only sixty-one have taken a chronic course. The good prognosis in acute catatonia is mainly due to this group (52, 101). At re-examination only six had reduced social adaptation, which was related to mental instability. It is noteworthy that the systematic, predominantly slowly developing catatonias for all types are not more than fifty-four, and thus less frequent than the periodic catatonias. A case report is presented.

No. 15001. Female, born 1920. An aunt had a periodic catatonia with a chronic course of illness. Two sisters had periodic catatonic attacks, but, like the patient, recovered.

Prior to psychosis the patient had a neurotic personality structure. In 1940, at the age of twenty, apparently without relation to any external event, she had difficulty in associations, and her interests centered only on religious problems. After some weeks the patient suddenly, one day, became excited and went in the nude around the town where she lived. A few days afterwards she was admitted to Gaustad Hospital.

In the hospital she presented a typical catatonic excitation, she spoke incoherently, and she heard voices coming from without as well as from her own ears. Emotionally she revealed a combination of ecstasy and perplexity. After a week the patient became quiet, and after three months stay in the hospital she could be discharged as not insane with the diagnosis of schizophrenia.

At re-examination in her home, the patient had been mentally healthy during an observation period of sixteen years. She had married in 1945 and was well adapted in all aspects.

Fünfgeld and *Leonhard* have described a group of *motility psychoses*, which are different from the catatonias. They are characterized by phases of akinesis and hypermotility (53, 101). We have placed ten patients in this group. The distinction between these psychoses and periodic catatonia or stupor-confusion psychoses are so subtle that they might as well be included in these groups. At re-examination three of them were so unstable that their social adaption was reduced. The following case may serve as an example.

No. 15399. Male, born 1922. A sister had epilepsy, and a half-sister had recovered from an attack of periodic catatonia.

The patient had a rather harmonious prepsychotic personality. In 1942 he suddenly became psychotic without any known external precipitating events. When shortly afterwards he was admitted to Gaustad Hospital, he was very excited, angry and aggressive. He took up the linoleum off the floor and tried to break the window. He was not able to give adequate answers to questions. The hyperkinetic excitation was followed by a more akinetic stage, and when the patient was inhibited he spoke very little and appeared emotionally blunted. After six months stay in the hospital he could be discharged as not insane with the diagnosis of schizophrenia.

In 1956 the patient was re-examined in his home. Of his dissease he remembered very little. He had been mentally healthy, had married in 1947 and lived happily with his wife.

The two groups of *hysteric pyschoses* are all found in the reactive group and are clearly non-schizophrenic. The first group of thirty cases corresponds to the psychogenic psychoses of *Färgeman* with disturbance of consciousness (54, 55). They are, according to *Kretschmer*, typical primitive reactions (91). The *confusional hysteric psychoses* have marked psychomotor symptoms, but nothing of the stiff and stereotyped movements of the catatonic patients. They should not be diagnosed as catatonias. In seventeen cases there was a reduced social adaptation due to neurotic or psychopathic traits. The following case may serve as an example.

> No. 16400. Female, born 1912. Two brothers had confusional hysteric psychoses.
>
> The patient had a sensitive premorbid personality. In 1940 she became depressed after the death of her fiancé, but did not need psychiatric treatment. One brother was treated in Gaustad Hospital in 1945. The other brother became suddenly psychotic in 1946 and was so excited and violent that four men had to hold him. The patient witnessed this, and afterwards could not sleep. In the course of a few days she developed a psychotic reaction similar to that of her brother. She was confused, talked incoherently, and was so excited and aggressive that it was necessary to keep her under restraint until she was admitted to the hospital.
>
> In Gaustad Hospital the patient had auditory hallucinations, psychomotor excitation and mannerisms, and was elated and ecstatic. After convulsive treatment she soon recovered, and could be discharged with the diagnosis of reactive psychosis.
>
> She was treated in another psychiatric hospital in 1956 for a depressive-confusional reactive psychosis. In 1957 she was re-examined in her home. No psychotic symptoms were found, but she was strongly neurotic with several psychosomatic complaints. Her working capacity was considerably lowered.

The group with eleven other hysteric psychoses is phenomenologically rather similar to the preceding. They can be considered as primitive reactions with clear consciousness. Their symptomatology represents dramatic tendency reactions, characteristic of hysteric personalities. In fact they can be regarded as an intermediate group between real psychoses and neurotic or psychopathic reactions. Five of them had clearly reduced social adaptation because of their abnormal personality traits. This is illustrated by the following case.

> No. 14940. Female, born 1904. No psychoses known in the family.
>
> The premorbid personality was classic hysteric. Since 1928 she had several hypochondriacal complaints, was treated in several

hospitals where no somatic basis for her symptoms could be found. As all her interests concentrated on various hypochondriacal complaints, she was admitted to Gaustad Hospital in 1940. She stayed over two years in the hospital, had headache, dyspepsia, lumbago, pains in the pharynx, and her symptoms varied greatly. On discharge she received the diagnosis of hysteriform reactive psychosis.

In 1948 the patient had a short period with confusion, excitement and visual hallucinations and was re-admitted to Gaustad Hospital. She was treated in the hospital during a half year and presented similar symptoms as during the first stay. In 1955-56 she was again treated for six months in Gaustad Hospital. This time she was childishly dependent with minor somatic complaints. The hospital diagnosis was a conversion neurosis.

When re-examined at home in 1959, the patient was strongly neurotic with lowered working capacity and psychosomatic complaints, but had succeeded in obtaining a marginal social adaptation.

In Anglo-Saxon literature much emphasis has been placed on groups labelled borderline states, abortive, ambulatory, latent, prepsychotic, masked, subclinical, pseudo-neurotic or pseudo-psychopathic schizophrenia (12, 15, 36, 66, 79, 112, 120, 142, 173). These conditions apparently represent, to a great extent, only various names for similar clinical conditions (15). There seems to be an agreement that these conditions do not develop schizophrenic deterioration (12, 66, 112). We had thirty-three cases which could be classified as *pseudo-neurotic* or *pseudo-psychopathic schizophrenia*.

In our opinion these states are poorly defined nosologically, and very difficult to delimit from other clinical entities. Having in mind that one of the original criteria for the diagnosis of these patients was their failure to respond to psychoanalytically oriented psychotherapy, the phenomenological clinical characteristics may vary greatly. According to *Astrup* and co-workers several such cases were admitted to Gaustad Hospital after unsuccessful psychotherapy. They responded well to institutional regimen, and can probably be treated successfully with practically oriented supportive psychotherapy. One cannot assume that pseudo-neurotic schizophrenias fail to respond to every type of psychotherapy. Neither does the poor effect of analytic therapy prove that psychogenic factors are of no importance for such conditions. Our experience would rather suggest that most cases are reactive psychoses, precipitated predominantly by psychogenic factors. They present mainly depressive, but also hysteric symptoms. We also stress that none of our 416 deteriorated schizophrenias developed from pseudo-neurotic schizophrenia to schizophrenic deterioration. All but four of the pseudo-neurotic and pseudo-psychopathic schizophrenias had so marked neurotic or psychopathic traits, that their social adaptation was reduced at re-examination.

There is good reason to agree with *Henri Ey,* that the pseudo-neurotic schizophrenias should not be included in the sensu strictorii schizophrenic group (46). This is demonstrated by the two following case histories.

Pseudo-neurotic Schizophrenia. No. 15750. Male, born 1915. An elder brother suffers from eccentric hebephrenia.

The patient had been nervous since childhood. After his elder brother became psychotic in 1932, the nervousness increased, and the disease of his brother laid a great strain on him. The patient was a student, but had for several years made practically no progress in his studies. He always felt tired, and had a lack of initiative. Some years before admission he became impotent, but thought that his sexual feelings were normal. Since 1935 he had dyspeptic complaints and felt strange sensations in his stomach. He consulted several doctors, but no somatic basis of his complaints could be found. In an internal medical department he noticed that the doctor wrote schizophrenia ? in the case report, and this made him very depressed.

The patient was admitted to Gaustad Hospital in 1944. He was depressed, felt dead in his body, could not see clearly and had pains in his stomach and head. In addition he suffered from a diffuse feeling of anxiety. In the hospital the patient received convulsive treatment, and after a month he could be discharged as slightly improved with the diagnosis of reactive psychosis.

When re-examined in 1957, the patient stated that he received psychoanalytic treatment from 1947 to 1949. He thought this treatment made it possible for him to finish his academic education. Although often feeling insecure and anxious, he had been able to do his work satisfactorily, had married and considered himself to be socially well-adapted.

Pseudo-psychopathic Schizophrenia. No. 15482. Male born 1911. No psychoses were known in the family.

The patient had shown psychopathic traits since childhood. At work he was unstable, and he drank immoderately. In 1941 he was imprisoned for theft. In prison he cut himself several times. Periodically he seemed confused, heard voices and felt persecuted. His persecutory delusions were rather vague and unsystematized. Because of suicidal attempts he was admitted to Gaustad Hospital in 1942. With institutional regimen his condition improved.

He was re-admitted in 1944 because of new suicidal attempts during imprisonment. This time institutional regimen was also deemed sufficient treatment.

In 1957 the patient was re-examined. He has since the last discharge from Gaustad Hospital been sentenced to prison, made suicidal attempts, and been treated twice in another phychiatric hospital. Now he was working on a farm. He stated that he had practically no contact with other people, felt they were speaking about him and looking at him. The patient also complained about being very anxious. Otherwise he had the typical psychopathic outward projecting tendency.

A group of fifty-five patients with *depersonalization psychoses* have been singled out. Phenomenologically depersonalization can be considered neither as a primitive reaction nor as affective, but in our material depersonalization is always accompanied by depressive or elated reactions, and in particular by depression. We think it justified to consider such psychoses as affective. Several authors have pointed out that depersonalization psychoses may be considered as a nosological entity, which should be separated from the schizophrenias (15, 56, 152, 165).

Some authors have argued that schizophrenia often starts as depersonalization psychoses. This opinion was not shared by *Bremer,* and not one of our 416 deteriorating schizophrenias started in this way (24). It is well known that depersonalization may be found in the most varied clinical states as well as in normal fatigue (1, 65, 117). A great deal of our chronic schizo-phrenics have presented depersonalization in the acute stage. Their depersonalization experiences regularly had a delusional character and were combined with other typical schizophrenic symptoms.

In the manic-depressive group the depersonalization experi-ences are apparently rather secondary to the basic mood changes. As to clinical recovery and social adaption they are as well off as the more typical manic-depressive forms (9 recovered and 7 improved).

The depersonalization states are more central in the clinical pictures of recovered schizophrenics and reactive psychoses. The patients feel as if they or their surroundings are changed, but are well aware that this is not true. As to risk of schizophrenic deter-ioration the prognoses is good. The disease is likely to take a pro-longed course, and at re-examination most of them are suffering from neurotic symptoms, so that with respect to social adaptation they could be classified as only improved (23 improved and 16 recovered).

Some of the recovered hebephrenics were found in this group (Table 18), and likewise some of the recovered schizophrenics coded as having affective blunting (Table 21). It is likely that in these cases an emotional indifference was interpreted as an affective flattening.

Other authors state that depersonalization psychoses are not so prognostically favorable as other types of affective psy-choses with respect to duration of illness and social adapta-tion (117, 152). In our experience this is most characteristic of the reactive psychoses, where only eight of twenty-five could be considered as recovered. A case report is presented.

No. 15547. Male, born 1924. The mother was nervous, and a half-brother was treated in a mental hospital with the diagnosis of psychopathia.

The patient had a neurotic personality structure. At the age of eighteen he started to sleep badly and felt that he could not control his thoughts. It was as if nature around him was changed, and he experienced an indefinable feeling of alteration within

himself. When one day he looked in the mirror he felt as if hypnotized by himself and started to ask who he was. He feared he was
becoming insane, and felt split up, as if two forces were fighting
within him.

The patient was treated in Gaustad Hospital from 4/20/43
to 8/17/45 and discharged as not insane. During the hospital stay
he made two attempts at suicide. No delusions or hallucinations
could be established, and he was adequate in his affects, taking
into consideration his great sufferings. He feared that he suffered
from schizophrenia, but the hospital diagnosis was one of a reactive
psychosis.

In 1956 the patient was re-examined in his home. Since discharge he had married and had succeeded very well in his work.
He often had "splitting" experiences, feeling as if his soul was
outside, observing the body. The derealization experiences had
passed. Previously the depersonalization feelings were accompanied
by great anxiety, but in later years he had overcome this anxiety.

In a group of *reactive depressions* we have placed forty-
three patients. The reactive depression represents a fairly well
defined entity. We refer to the descriptions of *Birnbaum, Lange,
Kielholz* and *Färgeman,* (18, 54, 55, 78, 93). Within our group
of reactive depressions there are several varieties. We find mostly
the psychogenic depressions of *Birnbaum* and *Lange* (18,93).
Some cases correspond to the psychoprovoked melancholiform
reactions of *Lange* and others to the exhaustion depressions of
Kielholz (78, 93).

As to differential diagnosis towards the manic-depressive
psychoses, main differences have been stressed in our previous
publication (8). Like *Lewis* we often found it difficult to distinguish the individual cases of reactive depressions from endogenous depression (103). Nevertheless, we agree with *Roth,* that
for the time being it seems unjustified to ignore in practice or
in scientific inquiry this distinction (152). At re-examinations
twenty-four had reduced social adaptation due to neurotic or psychopathic traits. A case history is presented.

No. 16392. Female, born 1918. No genetic loading of psychoses
was known.
Prior to psychosis the patient had a sensitive personality with

sthenic traits. She lived an unhappy life with a husband who drank and was brutal to her. Her husband had sexual relations with other women, and was at the same time very jealous of the patient. The family had no flat, and their two children lived with relatives. The patient herself had grown up in an orphanage, and feared that her children might also be placed in an orphanage.

After an attempt at suicide the patient was admitted to Gaustad Hospital in 1946. In the hospital she was markedly depressed, cried very much and had visual hallucinations. In the course of two months she gradually recovered without receiving convulsive treatment or other somatic therapies.

The patient was re-examined in her home in 1957. She had divorced her husband and lived together with her children. In 1954 she was treated in another psychiatric hospital for a depressive reaction similar to that in 1946. This time the depression was also precipitated by psychic conflicts. The patient was very neurotic with psychosomatic complaints, and her working capacity was considerably lowered.

Our last group is composed of sixty-seven *typical manic-depressive psychoses.* As seen from Table 4 this is the group which remains when the more atypical anxiety-ecstasy and depersonalization psychoses are subtracted. This group has the instability of mood, characteristic of manic-depressives in its pure form. The clinical picture is dominated by disturbances of the vital feelings, and a non-schizophrenic course of illness is practically certain. These cases correspond to the narrow definition of manic-depressive psychoses given by Kurt *Schneider* (155). Most of them belong to our series of acute affective psychoses, and they have all the characteristics of manic-depressive psychoses described in our former publication (8). At re-examination thirty-three had recovered, and thirty-four were so mentally unstable that they could only be classified as improved. The following case history is reported as typical.

No. 16689. Female, born 1906. Her grandfather, father and a brother suffered from manic-depressive psychosis.

The body build was pyknic and the premorbid personality was typically cycloid. At the early age of sixteen the patient had a minor manic period, but did not need hospital treatment. In the following years she had many manic and depressive periods. Her first admission to a mental hospital was in 1948, when she was admitted to Gaustad Hospital. No special precipitating factors could be established, and she had been quite balanced until fourteen days before admission when she became sleepless, restless and elated.

In the hospital the patient was a classical manic with flight of ideas, hyperactivity and increased self-esteem. She presented no delusions or hallucinations. After one and one-half months she could be discharged as improved.

The patient was re-examined in her home in 1957. Since 1948 she had gone through six manic periods. During the examination she appeared syntonic and balanced, received the examiner in a friendly manner, and had a good understanding of her own illness. Her enjoyment of life was quite satisfactory, and when healthy she used to be on good terms with other people. She thought that the psychotic periods came somewhat independently of external stress and were always preceded by fatigue, insomnia and apathy.

Chapter III

MORTALITY AND SUICIDES

Altogether 160 patients died during the period of observation. The following table surveys the extent to which the deceased were followed up five years or more (see Table 5).

TABLE 5

MORTALITY AND CLINICAL DIAGNOSIS

Clinical Diagnosis	Followed-up Less than 5 Years	Followed-up 5 Years or More	Total Deceased
Schizophrenia	32	49	81
Reactive psychoses	27	20	47
Manic-dperessive psychoses	20	12	32
Total	79	81	160

Among the schizophrenic eighty-one died. According to the general mortality rates for the population of Norway 1946-50, the expected number is thirty-three, which gives a relative death-rate of 2.5.

In the reactive group forty-seven died, as against an expected number of eight and a relative death-rate of 5.9. A high excess mortality was also found in the manic-depressives with thirty-two dead and a relative death-rate of 3.6.

After four years we should have expected that eight schizophrenics, two manic-depressives and four with reactive psychoses would have died. The actual figures were thirty-two, twenty and twenty-seven. Thus the excess mortality of all diagnostic sub-groups mainly occurred during the first four years after admission, and this was especially the case for the manic-depressives.

Ödegård has calculated the mortality rates for all first admissions to Norwegian mental hospitals during the years 1916 to 1949. The mortality was found to be around three to five times as high in the insane as in the general population. The excess mortality was highest during the first year of hospitalization, while chronic patients tended towards a normal mortality. The mortality was distinctly higher in manic-depressive insanity than in schizophrenia (125, 129, 130). Our findings correspond well with those of Ödegård. Ödegård found lower relative mortality in the reactive psychoses than in manic-depressive psychoses and schizophrenia. As only a small proportion of our deceased reactive psychoses died in mental hospitals, first admission statistics cannot demonstrate their excess mortality sufficiently. Another factor was that many of the followed-up recovered schizophrenics, of whom very few died, were diagnosed as reactive psychoses. They contribute to a lowering of the first admission mortality of reactive psychoses.

The next question was whether there were any sex differences. We had seventy-eight women who died, and eighty-two men. The relative death-rates were 2.1 for men and 3.6 for women. Ödegård found also relative excess mortality of the female sex.

Table 6 surveys the main causes of death in the three diagnostic categories (see table).

TABLE 6

CAUSES OF DEATH AND CLINICAL DIAGNOSIS

Clinical Diagnosis	Tuberculosis	Other Infections (Including Pneumonia)	Circulatory Diseases	Apoplexia	Cancer	Leucotomy	Suicides	Other Causes of Death	Insufficiently Known Causes of Death	Total
Schizophrenia	11	12	8	9	8	14	5	11	3	81
Reactive psychoses	8	2	13	2	7	2	8	4	1	47
Manic-depressive psychoses	0	8	7	5	4	1	3	3	1	32
Total	19	22	28	16	19	17	16	18	5	160

Leucotomy was the cause of death in seventeen cases, fourteen of whom were schizophrenics. If these fourteen therapeutically provoked deaths are subtracted, the excess mortality of the schizophrenics is considerably reduced.

Comparatively more reactive psychoses than schizophrenias died from tuberculosis. None of the manic-depressives died from tuberculosis. According to *Ödegård* all functional psychoses had an excess mortality of tuberculosis, and schizophrenia and manic-depressive psychoses had greater relative mortality than the reactive psychoses (129). The reason for the discrepancies may partly be the smallness of our sample. The epidemiological changes of tuberculosis in the general population as well as in the mental hospital population may also have acted differently upon the diagnostic groups.

Other infectious diseases were the most common cause of death in the endogenous psychoses, and in particular in the manic-depressive psychoses. This might support hypotheses that the endogenous psychoses are associated with a lowered resistance towards infections.

Considerably more affective psychotic than schizophrenics died from circulatory diseases. This corresponds to the findings of *Ödegård,* who pointed out that the schizophrenics may by protected by their less intensive emotional reactions and their physical inactivity (129). According to *Ödegård* apoplexy was also a relatively rare cause of death in schizophrenics, and our findings point in the same direction. *Ödegård* could confirm the findings of previous investigators, that cancer mortality is not higher in the insane (129). We found nineteen deaths, and the expected number was fifteen. For insufficiently known and other causes of death the expected number of deceased was thirteen, whereas we had twenty-three deaths.

There were sixteen suicides. The expected number should be one for the total material. The excess suicide rate was particularly great for the reactive psychoses. In chapter V is seen that attempts at suicide were as common in the reactive as in the manic-depressive psychoses. The manic-depressive had, according to chapter VI, considerably more relatives with suicidal tendencies than the reactive psychoses.

A possible explanation of these discrepancies may be that
the manic-depressives make determined attempts at suicide even
before the illness is recognized. This could account for the many
suicides among relatives of manic-depressives. When a manic-
depressive psychosis is diagnosed all efforts are made to protect
the patient against himself. When relapses occur, relatives as well
as doctors know that the patient must be closely watched until
the psychotic period has passed. In the reactive psychoses the
attempts at suicide may be more related to severe life experiences
than to constitutional predisposition. The attempts at suicide are
often demonstrative and are not taken so very seriously by relatives and doctors. Such precautions are, therefore, not taken to
protect them against suicide as in the case with the manic-depressives. Another factor is that psychotic periods in manic-depressives tend to be recognized by the usual precipitating symptoms, as, e.g., mood swings and sleep disturbances; and there is
practically no suicidal risk between the periods. Patients with
reactive psychoses are, as a rule, neurotic or psychopathic. For
this habitual state, hospitalization is not indicated. The ability to
tolerate life stress is reduced, and feelings of intolerable situations
may lead to suicides without anybody being able to prevent it.

Chapter IV

PROGNOSIS IN RELATION TO INDIVIDUAL CLINICAL FACTORS

1. PROGNOSIS AND DIAGNOSTIC CLASSIFICATION

Table 7 presents the hospital diagnosis made at the time of

TABLE 7

PROGNOSIS AND DIAGNOSTIC CLASSIFICATION

Outcome	Diagnosis of the Hospital							
	Reactive Psychoses							
	Schizo-phrenia	*Schizo-phrenia ?*	*Depressive*	*Paranoid*	*Hysteric*	*Confusional*	*Manic-depressive*	*Total*
Deteriorated schizophrenics	296	7	21	65	15	1	11	416
Improved schizophrenics	74	3	5	21	10	0	4	117
Recovered schizophrenics	65	12	13	18	20	3	0	131
Reactive psychoses	0	0	107	27	66	6	0	206
Manic-depressive psychoses	0	0	0	0	0	0	102	102
Total	435	22	146	131	111	10	117	972

discharge (see table). In acute schizophrenias and schizophreniform psychoses, the clinical outcome was practically the same for cases diagnosed as schizophrenia as for those diagnosed as reactive psychoses (68). In the total follow-up series 69 per cent of those with schizophrenic defects, had been diagnosed as schizophrenias. Only 15 per cent of the diagnosed schizophrenias had recovered. This shows that the diagnosis of schizophrenia was associated with small chances of recovery, but failed to predict schizophrenic defects very often. Among 398 patients diagnosed as reactive psychoses, 35 per cent have developed schizophrenic defects. This shows that the hospital's concept of reactive psychoses has been too broad. Out of 131 diagnosed as paranoid reactive psychoses, 66 per cent must be considered as certain schizophrenias according to the course of illness. One should be especially careful in diagnosing a paranoid reactive psychosis. When typical schizophrenic symptoms were present, these psychoses showed only 17 per cent recovered.

For the remaining patients diagnosed as reactive psychoses, the risk of schizophrenic defects was considerably smaller, with 18 per cent in depressive, 23 per cent in hysteriform, and 10 per cent in confusional psychoses; but if typical schizophrenic symptoms were present, the risks increased to respectively 67 (depressive), 56 (hysteriform) and 25 (confusional with only 4 cases) per cent.

In the group diagnosed as manic-depressive psychoses, 13 per cent developed schizophrenic defects. The diagnoses of manic-depressive psychoses had a relatively great reliability for predicting a small risk of schizophrenic deterioration.

There were 664 patients in the three schizophrenic outcome groups, and 20 per cent of them recovered, but half of the recovered were atypical, schizoaffective cases. We think that a concept of schizophrenia with 20 per cent recovered should not be too broad. This concept makes it also possible to establish groups of affective psychoses, where a very small risk of schizophrenic deterioration can be predicted. To diagnose as reactive psychoses such states which in the long run develop schizophrenic defects should be avoided.

2. PROGNOSIS OF DISEASE RELATED TO OBSERVATION PERIOD

We notice that the greatest proportion of the material has an observation period from ten to fourteen years. The average observation period was 12.3 years (see Table 8).

In the three observational groups the percentages of schizophrenic defects were respectively fifty-one, fifty--nine and fifty-two. As the longest observation period did not result in more schizophrenic defects than average for the material, a prolonga-

TABLE 8

PROGNOSIS AND OBSERVATION PERIOD

Outcome	Observation Period			
	5 - 9 Years	10 - 14 Years	15 - 22 Years	Total
Deteriorated schizophrenics	105	197	114	416
Improved schizophrenics	29	54	34	117
Recovered schizophrenics	38	47	46	131
Reactive psychoses	62	91	53	206
Manic-depressive psychoses	28	37	37	102
Total	262	426	284	972

tion of the observation period would probably not essentially change the percentages. In all three periods the percentage relationship between improved and deteriorated schizophrenics was practically the same. This implies that the distinction between improvement and deterioration is rather independent of the observation period. The variations in the distribution of the groups with a non-schizophrenic course of illness may be related to so many factors that we do not venture any conclusions.

3. PROGNOSIS AND SEX

From Table 9 it is seen that the material includes more

TABLE 9

PROGNOSIS AND SEX

Outcome	Male	Sex Female	Total
Deteriorated schizophrenics	214	202	416
Improved schizophrenics	64	53	117
Recovered schizophrenics	74	57	131
Reactive psychoses	71	135	206
Manic-depressive psychoses	28	74	102
Total	451	521	972

women than men (see Table 9). Reactive psychoses as well as manic-depressive psychoses were significantly more common in the female sex than the schizophrenias (P < 0.001 for both groups*). In the schizophrenic outcome groups there were practically as many women as men and no clearcut differences with regard to the course of illness. Other authors have similar findings for schizophrenia (15, 97).

4. PROGNOSIS AND AGE OF ONSET

Table 10 reveals that the age of onset is of very great import-

TABLE 10

PROGNOSIS AND AGE OF ONSET

Outcome	20 Years or Less	21 - 30 Years	Age at Onset 31 - 40 Years	40 Years	Total
Deteriorated schizophrenics	62	132	129	93	416
Improved schizophrenics	19	39	35	24	117
Recovered schizophrenics	19	50	43	19	131
Reactive psychoses	15	50	61	80	206
Manic-depressive psychoses	2	14	15	71	102
Total	117	285	283	287	972

ance for outcome (see table). In the group twenty years or less 69 per cent have developed schizophrenic defects, whereas above forty years only 41 per cent did so. This is mainly due to the preponderance of affective psychoses in the higher age groups.

In schizophrenia those with twenty-one to thirty years had the best outcome with 23 per cent recovered. Those above forty years had only 14 per cent recovered, and the differences between those age groups were statistically significant at the 0.05 level. Between thirty-one and forty years 21 per cent recovered and among those twenty years or less 19 per cent. Thus, schizophrenic

---

* The level of statistical significance is determined by the chi-square method, which in the following is used for statistical comparisons.

symptoms give slightly smaller chances of recovery in the oldest and youngest age groups. To judge from literature there is no agreement about the prognostic influence of age of onset (15, 27, 94, 97).

5. PROGNOSIS AND BODY TYPE

A pyknic body type was especially common among the manic-

TABLE 11

PROGNOSIS AND BODY TYPE

Outcome	Body Type				
	Incomplete Information	*Pyknic*	*Leptosome*	*Others or Uncharacteristic*	*Total*
Deteriorated schizophrenics	21	93	155	147	416
Improved schizophrenics	3	22	52	40	117
Recovered schizophrenics	2	21	45	63	131
Reactive psychoses	13	69	63	61	206
Manic-depressive psychoses	3	53	20	26	102
Total	42	258	335	337	972

depressives (see Table 11). In the reactive group a pyknic body type was also considerably more often found than in the three schizophrenic groups (P < 0.001).

A leptosomic body type was especially common in the improved schizophrenics, but practically as frequent in the deteriorated as in the recovered schizophrenics.

Most authors find that a pyknic body type protects against schizophrenic deterioration (27, 94, 97), but in our series of schizophrenics there are only 15 per cent recovered with pyknic body type as compared with 18 per cent with leptosome and 25 per cent with others or uncharacteristic body type. The improved schizophrenics, compared with the deteriorated included more with leptosome than pyknic body type (not significant). It appears that a pyknic body type in schizophrenic psychoses does not increase chances of recovery or improvement. The pyknic body type is only prognostically favorable because it is more common in the affective than in the schizophrenic psychoses (P < 0.001).

For our findings one must take the reservation that the coding of body type is based on clinical judgment without exact measurement.

6. PROGNOSIS AND PREPSYCHOTIC PERSONALITY

We have coded more personality traits than we have patients, because cases with mixed personality structures have been registered in two groups. (Also in some of the following tables more factors than patients are coded [see Table 12].)

TABLE 12

PROGNOSIS AND PREPSYCHOTIC PERSONALITY

Outcome	Prepsychotic Personality								
	Schizoid	*Sensitive*	*Self-assertive*	*Cycloid*	*Hysterical*	*Neurotic*	*Harmonious*	*Incomplete Information*	*Total*
Deteriorated schizophrenics	157	65	63	9	23	16	49	52	434
Improved schizophrenics	34	35	22	6	5	5	17	7	131
Recovered schizophrenics	26	39	20	8	7	14	28	7	149
Reactive psychoses	11	93	35	4	27	20	19	9	218
Manic-depressive psychoses	2	19	5	24	1	2	49	2	104
Total	230	251	145	51	63	57	162	77	1,036

Information is most frequently incomplete in the schizophrenic group. The reason for this is obviously that many of them have been sick for such a long time that it is difficult to establish what the prepsychotic personality has been.

For those with a schizoid personality the illness has taken a schizophrenic course in 83 per cent of the cases. It is very probable, however, that what we have considered as prepsychotic schizoid traits in a great many of the patients are really symptoms of an insidiously developing schizophrenic process. Such personality traits were considerably more frequent in the insidiously developing schizophrenias than in the acute cases (P < 0.001). The poor prognosis for schizoid prepsychotic personalities is, however, generally accepted by most authors (20, 27, 94, 97, 111).

A self-assertive personality was associated with schizophrenic defects in 59 per cent of the cases. These personalities were especially found among patients with paranoid defects, and it is probable that in several cases prodromals of paranoid schizophrenia have been falsely coded as self-assertive premorbid traits. This applies especially to the insidiously developing psychoses.

Harmonious and cycloid personalities were significantly more common in the manic-depressives than in the rest of the material (P < 0.001 for both personality types). As discussed in our study of acute affective psychoses, there is good reason to assume that a cycloid personality may often be a residual of minor manic-depressive periods (8). The great proportion of harmonious personalties indicates that the manic-depressive psychosis is not so much related to abnormal premorbid personality traits.

The reactive group has significantly more patients with sensitive (P < 0.001), hysteric (P < 0.001) personalities than the other outcome groups. This is easily understandable when one bears in mind that the reactive psychoses mostly occur in persons with personality deviations (8).

7. INTELLIGENCE AND PROGNOSIS

In schizophrenia inferior intelligence is prognostically very unfavorable with only 10 per cent recovered (see Table 13). This corresponds to the findings of other authors (15, 50, 61). One must have in mind that what is coded as low premorbid intelligence may in schizophrenics be effects of personality changes due to an insidious schizophrenic process. If the disease actually has started before puberty, information from school and relatives

TABLE 13

PROGNOSIS AND INTELLIGENCE

| | Intelligence | | | |
	Incomplete Information	*Below Average*	*Average or Above*	*Total*
Deteriorated schizophrenics	9	97	310	416
Improved schizophrenics	1	17	99	117
Recovered schizophrenics	1	12	118	131
Reactive psychoses	2	57	147	206
Manic-depressive psychoses	0	5	97	102
Total	13	188	771	972

may falsely point towards an inborn deficiency. We had, in fact, more persons with low intelligence among insidiously developing than among acute schizophrenics.

The manic-depressives had very few below average with respect to intelligence, as has been pointed out by other authors (80, 114, 161), but the reactive psychoses had a very great percentage below average. It is probable that low intelligence makes it more difficult to solve psychic conflicts, and in this way predisposes to reactive psychoses.

8. DURATION OF ILLNESS BEFORE ADMISSION

For the total material the duration of illness is of a decisive prognostic importance (see Table 14). In the group less than six months 37 per cent have developed schizophrenic defects, whereas in the group more than ten years 88 per cent have done so.

The reactive and manic-depressive psychoses have predominately lasted less than six months before admission.

In the schizophrenic group those with less than six months' duration had 37 per cent recovered. Only 5 per cent of the remaining recovered. It is concluded that, when the disease has lasted more than six months prior to admission, psychoses with schizophrenic symptoms have but a small chance of recovery. In these cases the recovery percentage is very similar to the process

TABLE 14

DURATION OF ILLNESS BEFORE ADMISSION

Outcome	< ½ Year	½ to 1 Year	1 to 2 Years	2 - 5 Years	5 - 10 Years	> 10 Years	Total
Deteriorated schizophrenics	130	60	42	78	51	55	416
Improved schizophrenics	66	18	11	14	5	3	117
Recovered schizophrenics	113	11	2	1	2	2	131
Reactive psychoses	141	31	13	9	7	5	206
Manic-depressive psychoses	87	7	5	2	0	1	102
Total	537	127	73	104	65	66	972

schizophrenias of *Langfeldt* (39, 94). The chances of improvement are also reduced when the disease has lasted for more than six months, with only 15 per cent improved among schizophrenic defects as compared with 34 per cent in the acute cases.

9. PROGNOSIS ACCORDING TO TYPE OF ONSET

The type of onset we have coded regardless of the duration

TABLE 15

PROGNOSIS ACCORDING TO TYPE OF ONSET

Outcome	Acute Onset Without Prodromal Symptoms	Acute Onset After Prodromal Symptoms	Sub-acute Onset	Insidious Onset With Periodic Exacerbations	Insidious Onset Without Periodic Exacerbations	Total
				Onset of Disease		
Deteriorated schizophrenics	32	64	120	80	120	416
Improved schizophrenics	18	36	29	20	14	117
Recovered schizophrenics	40	57	23	7	4	131
Reactive psychoses	94	34	45	20	13	206
Manic-depressive psychoses	56	13	25	7	1	102
Total	240	204	242	134	152	972

of illness before admission (see Table 15). It is seen from the table that a really acute onset without prodromal symptoms is prognostically very favorable, with only 21 per cent developing schizophrenic defects. On the other hand, the illness took a schizophrenic course in 88 per cent of those with an insidious onset without periodic exacerbations. Whereas 64 per cent of the affective psychoses had an acute onset, only 37 per cent of the schizophrenics had an acute onset.

In the schizophrenic groups the percentages of recovered gradually decreased from 45 per cent in those with acute onset without prodromal symptoms to 3 per cent in those with insidious onset without periodic exacerbations. The two groups with acute onsets had 39 per cent recovered as compared with 8 per cent in the remaining.

One must be aware that only twenty of the schizophrenics with acute onset had been ill for more than 6 months prior to admission. This implies that in cases with acute onset hospital admission is seldom delayed.

In conclusion, the type of onset is an extremely important prognostic factor. This corresponds to the findings of other authors (15, 27, 76).

10. PRECIPITATING FACTORS AND PROGNOSIS

Many patients show combinations of several factors and, therefore, our table contains more precipitating factors than patients (see Table 16).

No known precipitating factors were considerably more common in the deteriorated schizophrenics than in the other outcome groups (P < 0.001). In fact 74 per cent of those without any known precipitating factors had developed schizophrenic defects. We assume that quite often we have been unable to discern precipitating factors because the patients have been too ill to tell about the sufferings they have had. Experiences with group therapy and conditional reflex experiments may support this assumption. A characteristic trait in the group behavior of many schizophrenics was a difficulty in expressing their reactions to problems in their lives, so that even if the case histories revealed severe mental trauma, they paid no attention to these stresses.

TABLE 16
PRECIPITATING FACTORS AND PROGNOSIS
Precipitating Factors

Outcome	Acute Mental Trauma	Prolonged Mental Conflicts				Social Misery Isolation	Somatic Disease Childbirth	Intoxication Mostly Alcoholic	No Special Factors Mentioned	Total
		Parental	Sexual	Religious	Others					
Deteriorated schizophrenics	31	7	72	5	56	21	42	16	201	451
Improved schizophrenics	8	6	22	0	30	2	19	5	38	130
Recovered schizophrenics	11	6	35	5	28	3	25	10	26	149
Reactive psychoses	67	4	64	5	47	6	51	11	26	281
Manic-depressive psychoses	21	2	10	0	15	0	33	2	34	117
Total	138	25	203	15	176	32	170	44	325	1,128

It seems that this attitude can be correlated with a lacking capacity to verbalize motor performances in the test situation (7). Also, no known precipitating factors were more common in the manic-depressives than in reactive psychoses (P < 0.001). This factor is a common trait in the endogenous in contrast to the reactive psychoses.

In the small group with social misery or isolation, the majority have also developed schizophrenic defects. Such factors are extremely common in our functional psychoses. For the majority not coded there was every reason to assume that social misery or isolation was secondary to the mental disorder. This may be so in the cases which we have coded in this category.

We found significantly less schizophrenic defects than average for the total material in patients with such clear-cut exogenic factors as acute mental trauma (P < 0.001), somatic disease and childbirth (P < 0.001). Alcoholic and other intoxications were not prognostically favorable. This factor was more common in schizophrenics than in affective psychoses.

Acute mental trauma was more common in the reactive psychoses, (P < 0.001) and somatic disease or childbirth more common in the manic-depressive psychoses (P < 0.001) than in the other outcome groups.

For the prolonged mental conflicts it may be difficult to decide what should be regarded as causes or as symptoms of a beginning mental disorder. This applies especially to the more insidiously developing schizophrenic psychoses.

Parental conflicts have been coded only in twenty-five cases, and mainly for younger patients who have had difficult relations with parents at the period before outbreak of the disease. One-half of them developed schizophrenic defects. We are aware that difficult childhood experiences may have played a great role for many of our patients without directly precipitating the outbreak of the psychosis.

Religious conflicts have been coded in few cases, and gave 33 per cent with schizophrenic defects. Religious megalomania or religious feelings of guilt or sin are often found among our patients, but as a rule only expressing delusions after outbreak of the illness.

Sexual conflicts were common in our material and revealed 46 per cent with schizophrenic defects. It was noticed that sexual conflicts were more common in the reactive psychoses than in the other outcome groups (P < 0.02), and, in particular, more common than in the manic-depressives (P < 0.01).

Other prolonged mental conflicts gave 49 per cent with schizophrenic defects, which is practically the same as for sexual conflicts. Like sexual conflicts these conflicts were also more frequent in the reactive psychoses than in the manic-depressives.

For the three schizophrenic groups the prognosis is best in those with clearly demonstrable exogenic factors such as intoxication with 32 per cent, somatic disease or childbirth with 29 per cent and acute mental trauma with 22 per cent recovered. The group with prolonged mental conflicts had 27 per cent recovered, whereas those with no precipitating factors had only 10 per cent recovered. Like most other authors we find that exogenic factors are prognostically favorable in schizophrenia (15, 94, 97). An absence of precipitating factors is, however, to a great extent associated with long duration of illness, being significantly more common in insidiously developing than in acute schizophrenias (P < 0.001). In the cases of long duration it is especially difficult to establish which stress is precipitating or resulting from the psychotic reaction.

11. PROGNOSIS AND TREATMENT

In the total material those with no somatic treatment have the smallest percentage of schizophrenic defects (44 per cent)

TABLE 17

PROGNOSIS AND TREATMENT

Outcome	Treatment			No Shock Treatment	Total
	Convulsive	Insulincoma	Leucotomy		
Deteriorated schizophrenics	331	53	91	85	560
Improved schizophrenics	88	11	19	29	147
Recovered schizophrenics	113	7	0	18	138
Reactive psychoses	109	2	9	96	216
Manic-depressive psychoses	74	1	5	28	108
Total	715	74	124	256	1,169

(see Table 17). The reason for this is that the affective psychoses, and, in particular, the reactive psychoses, did not need somatic treatment to a great extent. In the three schizophrenic groups only 14 per cent of those without treatment recovered. The "untreated" schizophrenias are undoubtedly a selected material. Some recovered spontaneously before any treatment was instigated, but the majority were long standing cases where somatic treatment was not expected to benefit the patients (72 per cent had more than 6 months duration).

Among patients given convulsive treatment 59 per cent developed schizophrenic defects. Among the schizophrenics 21 per cent recovered. All patients treated with insulin coma or leucotomy had previously received convulsive treatment, or convulsive treatment was combined with coma. It is remarkable that only 10 per cent of the schizophrenics have recovered with additional insulin coma.

Leucotomy cannot be expected to give real recoveries as this method, as a rule, has been the last resort in "hopeless" cases and gives sequelae of the operation. There is a possibility that, in some of the improved ones, personality changes after operation have been misinterpreted as schizophrenic residuals. In those with no convulsive treatment the improved made up 25 per cent of the schizophrenic defects, while the improved leucotomized were only 17 per cent, and 83 per cent were classified as deteriorated. Among patients treated with convulsive treatment, the improved were 21 per cent of the schizophrenic defects. The leucotomized cases have the smallest proportion of improved schizophrenias, and the long term prognosis of this therapy has proved very poor. A similar conclusion could be drawn by *Christensen* in a material of leucotomized schizophrenics from Norwegian Hospitals (28).

12. PROGNOSIS AND CLINICAL SYNDROMES

Often the same patient has presented two or more clinical syndromes, so that we have considerably more syndromes than patients (see Table 18).

TABLE 18

PROGNOSIS AND CLINICAL SYNDROMES

Outcome	*Clinical Syndrome at Onset*							
	Depression	*Excitation*	*Confusion*	*Paranoid*	*Hebephrenic*	*Catatonic*	*Hysteriform*	*Total*
Deteriorated schizophrenics	36	22	14	311	145	84	6	618
Improved schizophrenics	13	12	10	94	20	35	1	185
Recovered schizophrenics	20	25	13	105	7	51	1	222
Reactive psychoses	126	54	75	73	0	0	25	353
Manic-depressive psychoses	63	44	5	11	0	0	3	126
Total	258	157	117	594	172	170	36	1,504

The hebephrenic syndrome was prognostically very unfavorable with only 4 per cent recovered and 12 per cent improved schizophrenics, whereas the remaining 84 per cent deteriorated. Paranoid syndromes gave 68 per cent and catatonic syndromes 70 per cent with schizophrenic defects. The remaining syndromes give only 19 to 21 per cent with schizophrenic course of illness. In manic-depressive psychoses depression (P < 0.001), excitation (P < 0.001), and in reactive psychoses depression (P < 0.001), excitation (P < 0.001), confusion (P < 0.001), and hysteriform syndromes (P < 0.001) were significantly more common than in the remaining outcome groups.

In the three schizophrenic outcome groups excitation and confusion were most favorable with respectively 42 and 35 per cent recovered. Then followed the catatonic syndrome with 30 per cent and depression with 29 per cent. Catatonic syndromes are not especially less favorable than affective and confusional syndromes in the schizophrenic psychoses. Recovered and improved cases with catatonic syndromes are all periodic catatonias or mixed paranoid-catatonic states, characterized by acute onset and periodic course of illness. These states may be pathogenetically quite different from the systematic catatonias, which predominantly develop insidiously and present the most severe types of schizophrenic deterioration. The paranoid syndromes gave twenty-one and the hebephrenic 4 per cent recovered. The hebephrenic syndrome is, however, coded only where a flattening of the affect is found. As a rule such psychoses have an insidious course of illness, and 136 of the 172 hebephrenic had been ill for more than six months prior to admission.

13. PROGNOSIS AND INITIAL SYMPTOMS

Change of personality was prognostically very unfavorable with 88 per cent developing schizophrenic defects (see Table 19). One must have in mind that this symptom cannot, as a rule, be established before the illness has lasted for a considerable period. Also impulsivity and tantrums, vagrancy, restlessness, ideas of reference, jealousy and suspiciousness are strongly linked up with a schizophrenic outcome. These symptoms often set in insidiously and are associated with change of personality and were significantly less common in acute than in insidiously de-

TABLE 19

PROGNOSIS AND INITIAL SYMPTOMS

Outcome	*Transitory Periods*	*Change of Personality*	*Depressive Traits*	*Neurasthenic Traits*	*Ideas of Reference Suspicious Jealous*	*Impulsive Tantrums*	*Vagrancy Restlessness*	*Religious or Philo-sophical Preoccupation*	*No special Initial Symptoms Mentioned*	*Total*
Deteriorated schizophrenics	68	160	51	52	202	56	26	16	23	654
Improved schizophrenics	21	31	22	14	48	9	4	4	4	157
Recovered schizophrenics	28	24	28	26	40	6	7	4	11	174
Reactive psychoses	69	1	70	59	31	13	4	2	30	279
Manic-depressive psychoses	36	0	42	10	10	0	0	0	16	114
Total	222	216	213	161	331	84	41	26	84	1,378

veloping schizophrenias (P < 0.001). Their prognostic importance is, to a great extent, a function of long standing illness without markedly overt psychotic traits.

Transitory periods, no special initial symptoms and depressive and neurasthenic traits are associated with a non-schizophrenic course of illness in the majority of our patients. These initial symptoms are significantly more common in the affective than in the schizophrenic outcome groups (P < 0.001 for all comparisons).

In the three schizophrenic outcome groups impulsivity and tantrums, change of personality, ideas of reference, suspiciousness, and jealousy were prognostically unfavorable, with 8 to 14 per cent recovered. Most favorable were depressive, neurasthenic traits or no special initial symptoms with 28 to 29 per cent recovered. The latter symptoms were predominantly found in the acute schizophrenias.

14. PSYCHOMOTOR SYMPTOMS AND PROGNOSIS

For the total material inhibition was most closely associated with a favorable prognosis (24 per cent schizophrenic defects) (see Table 20). Great percentages of schizophrenic defects were remarkable for groups with no psychomotor symptoms (77 per

TABLE 20

PSYCHOMOTOR SYMPTOMS AND PROGNOSIS

Outcome	Psychomotor Symptoms									Total
	Inhibition	*Blocking*	*Stupor*	*Excitation*	*Mannerism*	*Agitation Restlessness*	*Negativism*	*Varying*	*No Psychomotor Disturbances Mentioned*	
Deteriorated schizophrenics	36	66	27	136	53	47	37	13	142	557
Improved schizophrenics	14	16	14	37	15	15	10	2	22	145
Recovered schizophrenics	17	24	14	80	13	5	12	2	15	182
Reactive psychoses	87	5	12	88	6	25	5	4	33	265
Manic-depressive psychoses	59	2	5	43	0	31	5	2	0	147
Total	213	113	72	384	87	123	69	23	212	1,296

cent) and such predominantly catatonic symptoms as mannerisms (78 per cent), negativism (68 per cent), blocking (73 per cent), and stupor (57 per cent). Inhibition, agitation, and restlessness were significantly more common in the affective than in the schizophrenic outcome groups (P < 0.001).

In the three schizophrenic outcome groups the percentages for recovery were for excitation 32, inhibition 25, stupor 25, negativism 20 and blocking 23 per cent. For the remaining symptoms the recovery rates varied between 8 and 16 per cent, with the worst outcome in cases without predominant psychomotor symptoms. It seems that the more violent are the psychomotor symptoms, the better is the prognosis. Lack of psychomotor symptoms was significantly more unfavorable as to recovery (P < 0.001). Other authors record similar experiences (101, 107).

15. PROGNOSIS IN RELATION TO EMOTIONAL SYMPTOMS

When we consider the total material, emotional blunting was prognostically most unfavorable with 94 per cent developing schizophrenic defects (see Table 21). The poor outcome demonstrates clearly that this symptom can be regarded as typical schizophrenic.

TABLE 21

PROGNOSIS IN RELATION TO EMOTIONAL SYMPTOMS

Outcome	*Depression*	*Elation, Euphoria, Ecstasy*	*Perplexity*	*Anxiety*	*Affective Instability*	*Emotional Blunting*	*Total*
			Affective Traits				
Deteriorated schizophrenics	110	93	63	21	117	206	610
Improved schizophrenics	39	39	25	6	23	39	171
Recovered schizophrenics	39	59	36	13	16	15	178
Reactive psychoses	148	34	15	47	34	0	278
Manic-depressive psychoses	68	42	14	32	4	0	160
Total	404	267	153	119	194	260	1,397

Anxiety was most favorable with 77 per cent recovered and significantly more common in affective than in schizophrenic outcome groups ($P < 0.001$). Depression was also more common in affective than in schizophrenic psychoses ($P < 0.001$) and revealed 63 per cent recoveries. Elation, euphoria and ecstasy were seen as often in affective as in schizophrenic psychoses, and the percentage of recovery was 51. Perplexity was more often found in the schizophrenic than in the affective outcome groups ($P < 0.001$), and 58 per cent developed schizophrenic defects.

In the three schizophrenic outcome groups emotional blunting and affective instability were very unfavorable with respectively 6 and 10 per cent recovered. "Affective instability" indicates that the patients had outbursts of rage, irritability and sudden unmotivated mood-swings from one day to another. These emotional disturbances could not phenomenologically be considered as affective blunting, but clearly had the character of an inappropriate affect, and occurred predominantly in the paranoid cases. Although prognostically unfavorable, affective instability is too difficult to distinguish from other emotional disturbances to be used as a diagnostic criterion. With the restricted definition we have given for affective blunting (68), this symptom is fairly reliable for predicting a poor outcome. An emotional blunting can usually not be established unless the patient has been ill for a considerable time, and 197 of the 260 coded as having emotional blunting had been psychotic more than six months prior to admission.

Elation, euphoria, ecstasy, perplexity and anxiety were most favorable with between 29 and 33 per cent recovered. Then followed depression with 21 per cent. It was remarkable that although perplexity (*"Ratlosigkeit"*) is supposed to be typical of schizophrenia, this symptom was in the schizophrenic groups more favorable than depression.

16. PROGNOSIS AND DELUSIONAL CONTENT

In chapter II we have described certain delusions as typical of schizophrenia (see Table 22). These were fantastic ideas of jealousy with eighty-eight, ideas of high descent with eighty-four, fantasy lover with eighty-two, non-religious megalomania (such as king, Stalin, Hitler) with eighty, and religious megalomania (such as Christ or prophets) with 68 per cent developing schizophrenic defects. These symptoms have, in fact, proved to be very strongly linked up with a schizophrenic course of illness.

Persecution and ideas of reference were also rather unfavorable, with respectively 69 and 65 per cent resulting in schizophrenic defects. These symptoms were, however, found in so many typical reactive psychoses that they cannot be considered as characteristic of schizophrenia.

In the total material absence of delusions gave thirty-nine, guilt and inferiority thirty and hypochondria forty-two per cent schizophrenic defects. All those symptoms were more common in the affective than in the schizophrenic outcome groups (P < 0.001 for all comparisons).

TABLE 22
PROGNOSIS AND DELUSIONAL CONTENT

Outcome	Guilt Inferiority	Hypochondria	Ideas of Reference	Persecution	Revindication	Megalomania				Fantastic Ideas of Jealousy	No Delusions Established	Total
						Religious	Other Forms	Fantasy Lover	Ideas of High Descent			
Deteriorated schizophrenics	36	53	113	225	13	57	41	35	14	32	69	688
Improved schizophrenics	13	18	29	63	6	22	16	14	2	4	11	198
Recovered schizophrenics	14	21	35	60	2	28	11	9	2	3	20	205
Reactive psychoses	38	54	37	54	12	0	0	0	0	0	79	274
Manic-depressive psychoses	60	22	4	12	1	9	3	2	1	2	25	141
Total	161	168	218	414	34	116	71	60	19	41	204	1,506

In the three schizophrenic groups the percentage of recovery varies between 26 for religious megalomania and 8 per cent for fantastic ideas of jealousy. The typical schizophrenic delusions gave recovery in 43 to 22 per cent in the series of acute schizophrenias and schizophreniform psychoses (68). In the present material the recovered cases, with five exceptions, had a duration of illness of less than six months prior to admission. Of the remaining long standing cases with typical schizophrenic delusions only 3 per cent recovered. The comparatively good prognosis of religious megalomania was due to a frequent occurrence in the acute schizoaffective states, where it was not possible to predict whether the individual patient would develop schizophrenic deterioration.

17. DISTURBANCE OF THINKING

Passivity and symbolism (disturbance of symbolization) were in the acute series considered as typical schizophrenic symptoms (68) (see Table 23). In the total material these symptoms give respectively 80 and 81 per cent with a schizophrenic course of illness, which clearly demonstrates the schizophrenic nature of these symptoms.

TABLE 23

DISTURBANCE OF THINKING

Outcome	Disturbance of Thinking						Total
	Flight of Ideas	Incoherence	Depersonalization	Passivity	Symbolism	No Mention of Thought Disturbance	
Deteriorated schizophrenics	6	89	138	211	140	78	662
Improved schizophrenics	3	28	54	66	40	14	205
Recovered schizophrenics	6	44	63	64	36	21	234
Reactive psychoses	3	25	31	0	0	151	210
Manic-depressive psychoses	35	9	19	7	5	44	119
Total	53	195	305	348	221	308	1,430

Then follows depersonalization with 63 per cent and incoherence with 60 per cent developing schizophrenic defects. Flight of ideas is prognostically favorable. but nevertheless with 17 per cent turning out as certain schizophrenias. This symptom is considerably more common in the manic-depressives than in other outcome groups ($P < 0.001$). Absence of disturbance of thinking was also prognostically favorable (70 per cent recovered), and more common in the reactive psychoses than in other groups ($P < 0.001$).

In the three schizophrenic outcome groups symbolism showed the worst prognosis with 17 per cent recovered. Then followed passivity and absence of thought disturbance with 19 per cent and depersonalization with 25 per cent recovered.

It should be noted that in several hebephrenic and catatonic cases no thought disturbances were recorded, and a diagnosis of schizophrenia could mainly be established on the basis of personality changes, emotional blunting and catatonic symptoms. Such cases mostly developed insidiously, and tended to result in severe deterioration. Compared with the rest of the material, the improved made up a minor percentage of the deteriorated schizophrenics in those with no thought disturbance.

Depersonalization has been considered by us as a typical schizophrenic symptom, and is often associated with passivity and other mental automatisms. In the affective psychoses we had fifty cases with affectively colored (mainly depressive) depersonalization. The "as if" feeling was typical of affective psychoses, but in schizophrenics was mostly replaced by overt psychotic experiences of changes of own person and surroundings. These experiences include apersonalization and transitivism, which are considered by *Bleuler* to be characteristic of schizophrenia (19). Though *Langfeldt* has considered depersonalization as a process symptom, his case histories show that this refers to delusional types of depersonalization (94). *Fish* considers it unfortunate that Scandinavian authors tend to use the term depersonalization to designate delusional experiences of control from outside (52). In this way depersonalization covers too different clinical states, and, as shown in cases of *Bremer,* may induce false predictions of schizophrenic deterioration in affectively colored depersonalization states (24). We could stress that only the delusional types of depersonalization should be regarded as typical schizophrenic.

Flight of ideas and incoherence were prognostically most favorable with respectively 40 and 27 per cent recovered. Incoherence occurs in clinically rather different types. In the defect schizophrenias incoherence is to a great extent a sign of long-standing thought disorder. Most of the recovered cases were acute psychoses with violent psychomotor excitement or disturbances of consciousness. Incoherence was also noted in twenty-five reactive psychoses with clouded consciousness. As incoherence occurs often in reactive psychoses, and furthermore is not so bound up with other schizophrenic automatisms, we would not consider this symptom as typical schizophrenic. But we can confirm the traditional opinion that incoherence with clear consciousness in insidiously developing schizophrenias is prognostically unfavorable (6 per cent recovered).

18. PROGNOSIS AND HALLUCINOSIS

Sexual and other haptic hallucinations as well as the special forms of auditory hallucinations we have considered as typical of

TABLE 24
PROGNOSIS AND HALLUCINATIONS

Outcome	Hallucinations							
					Haptic			
	Auditory	*Auditory Special Forms*	*Olfactory, Gustatory*	*Visual*	*Sexual*	*Others*	*Without Hallucination*	*Total*
Deteriorated schizophrenics	305	73	44	99	42	130	78	771
Improved schizophrenics	84	14	4	26	6	30	22	186
Recovered schizophrenics	99	24	13	34	6	26	23	225
Reactive psychoses	77	0	4	38	0	0	118	237
Manic-depressive psychoses	44	1	10	21	1	5	48	130
Total	609	112	75	218	55	191	289	1,549

schizophrenia (68). Schizophrenic defects develop in respectively 87, 84, and 78 per cent of cases with such symptoms (see Table 24).

Ordinary auditory hallucinations showed 64, olfactory and gustatory 64, visual 57 and absence of hallucinations 35 per cent with a schizophrenic course of illness. Ordinary auditory hallucinations were more common in the schizophrenic than in the affective groups (P < 0.01), whereas no hallucinations were frequent in the affective psychoses (P < 0.001). It is noted that the special forms of auditory hallucinations gave significantly more schizophrenic defects than the ordinary auditory hallucinations (P < 0.01).

In the schizophrenic groups the percentages of recovery varied from 22 per cent for special forms of auditory, olfactory, gustatory, and visual hallucinations to 11 per cent for sexual hallucinations. Among those with no hallucinations 19 per cent recovered.

Chapter V

SOCIAL FACTORS IN
FUNCTIONAL PSYCHOSES

1. INTRODUCTION

The purpose of this chapter is to analyze the extent to which the various groups of catamnestically verified psychoses differ with regard to social factors.

The analysis has been limited to personally seen cases. The reason for this is primarily that information about social factors at re-examination is rather scarce in the case of patients followed up. The clinical outcome of the illness is best ascertained in these cases. Altogether we have included 555 patients in our study of social factors.

There is every reason to assume that the sample is representative of the affective psychotics who were for the most part located in their homes and personally examined. The same is the case for the recovered and improved schizophrenics. The deteriorated schizophrenics seen in their homes are, according to Chapter II, a selection of mildly deteriorated cases, whereas those re-examined in Gaustad Hospital have a great proportion of severe defects. In both these groups the severely deteriorated make up 35 per cent, whereas the severely deteriorated are 37 per cent in the total material. Thus the personally seen cases should be quite a representative sample with respect to the severity of schizophrenic deterioration.

For the literature concerning social psychiatric problems we would refer to previous work of *Astrup* (5, 6). *Ödegård* has analyzed influences of social factors upon psychiatric morbidity in Norway in great detail. To some extent it is possible to compare his extensive statistical data with the findings in our comparatively small clinical sample. With the first admission statistics from Norway the statistical analysis was based on approximately 50,000 cases, so that detailed subgrouping with regard to social factors was possible (6, 138, 139). Several social factors have been analyzed by a method similar to that used in the previous study by *Ödegård* of delayed admissions (136). Several of the delayed admissions were functional psychoses, which are included in the present material.

We have laid great emphasis on comparing various social factors before first admission and at re-examination. In this way we can obtain an idea of how social factors affect prognosis, and on the other hand, how the course of illness is related to such factors after discharge.

As we have purposely avoided analysis of very complex sociological or psychological phenomena, we have not attempted to study the prognostic importance of living conditions in childhood. Previous studies by *Nielsen from* Gaustad Hospital did not show particular characteristics of the childhood of schizophrenics, and our case material did not make it possible to penetrate deeper into this problem (119). We are also aware that team-work by psychiatrists, sociologists, psychologists, and social workers may be a requisite for elucidating such complex phenomena as living conditions in childhood.

Our study has been limited to such factors as clinical psychiatrists reliably may evaluate on the basis of the case history and the personal interview at re-examination. Only social differences between various clinical outcome groups were dealt with, and it was not deemed necessary to compare with a material of "normals." But to some extent we may make adequate comparisons with the official population statistics of Norway.

2. WORKING CAPACITY

Pollock, Malzberg and *Fuller* have mentioned that schizophrenics had difficulty holding jobs before their illness (145). *Aldrich* and *Coffin* found in a follow-up study that in schizophrenia a good prognosis is correlated with a good occupational history (2). In their detailed study of prognosis in schizophrenia, *Wirt* and *Simon* write that those with a poor prognosis had poor work history throughout life (171). For delayed admissions *Ödegård* showed that a working ability helped to keep a psychiatric patient out of hospital (136). *Harris et al* found that patients who were judged to be well by social standards (earning their own living and independent) were likewise assessed by clinical standards (62). *Brown et al* reported an important relationship between employment and success or failure in post hospital adjustment (25).

From the preceding we considered it likely that our clinical outcome groups would differ with regard to working capacity before admission as well as at re-examination. The results of our comparisons are presented in the following table (see Table 25).

In the group with good working capacity we have included patients who have been able to do their work satisfactorily. In the group *good but unstable* are patients who can do their jobs but cannot succeed in keeping jobs for long periods. We have limited the group with *lowered capacity* to such patients who definitely fail to come up to working standards in their profession. There are very few who have not been working before they became psychotic.

At re-examination we have placed patients in public care in a separate group as they cannot be compared with the self-supporting patients. Several of the 118 chronic schizophrenics in Gaustad Hospital are able to do quite responsible work within the hospital and the same is true of some patients in family care.

When we compare the different schizophrenic outcome groups before admission, there is a clear-out correlation between a good prognosis and a good prepsychotic working capacity. Among recovered schizophrenics 82 per cent and among deteriorated schizophrenics in Gaustad Hospital only 56 per cent had a good prepsychotic working capacity. The differences are statistically significant at the 0.001 level.

The manic-depressives had the best working capacity before admission (85 per cent good). Those with reactive psychoses had working capacity similar to that of improved schizophrenics and chronic schizophrenics outside mental hospitals (approximately 65 per cent good).

At re-examination as many as thirteen chronic schizophrenics

TABLE 25

WORKING CAPACITY BEFORE ADMISSION AND AT RE-EXAMINATION

Working Capacity Before Admission and at Re-examination	Chronic Schizophrenics in Gaustad Hospital		Chronic Schizophrenics Outside Hospitals		Improved Schizophrenics		Recovered Schizophrenics		Manic-depressive Psychoses		Reactive Psychoses		Total	
	Before adm.	At re-ex.	Before adm.	At re-ex.	Before adm.	At re-ex.	Before adm.	At re-ex.	Before adm.	At re-ex.	Before adm.	At re-ex.	Before adm.	At re-ex.
Good	56		63	17	66	38	82	85	85	62	65	48	68	40
Good, but unstable	34		23	14	26	25	14	6	14	18	24	21	23	13
Lowered	10		10	33	7	28	4	9	1	8	9	21	8	16
Not working		100	4	20	1	8	0	0	0	5	2	7	1	6
In public care				16		1	0	0	0	7	0	3	0	25
Total	100	100	100	100	100	100	100	100	100	100	100	100	100	100
No. of cases	118	118	75	75	86	86	96	96	61	61	119	119	555	555

and thirty-three improved schizophrenics had a good working capacity. The improved schizophrenics had only slightly fewer persons with good working capacity than those with reactive psychoses. Manic-depressive patients had a greater proportion of good workers than reactive psychoses and significantly more than the improved schizophrenics ($P < 0.01$). But the recovered schizophrenics succeeded best in work, and have even more good workers at re-examination than before admission. The recovered schizophrenics had a significantly greater proportion of good workers than the affective psychoses ($P < 0.001$).

It was surprising how patients with schizophrenic defects often struggled to support themselves. This can be illustrated by a few examples.

No. 16680. Male, born 1911, treated in the hospital in 1948 and re-examined in his home in 1956. He was then extremely eccentric with affective flattening. Although he had a technical education, he struggled with heavy unskilled work on the docks. He complained about feeling very tired after the working day. Nevertheless he spent his leisure time studying languages and mercantile topics through correspondence courses. His hope was to educate himself better, so that he might obtain more qualified work. Coming from the middle class, he, and especially his relatives, considered his fellow workers as too vulgar for him.

No. 17140. Female, born 1906, treated in Gaustad Hospital in 1949, 1951, and 1956. In 1959 she was re-examined. She suffered from a paranoid schizophrenia with strongly affect-laden delusions. After the last discharge she had been able to obtain a good apartment for herself. She found work in a baker's firm and was entrusted with managing a branch with two assistants. The employer was very satisfied with her work, as the net profit of the branch increased and everything was kept in exemplary order. The patient had small personal needs, practically only worked and slept, and had saved up a considerable amount of money. In the hospital she had taken part in a group led by the examiner. During group psychotherapy it was emphasized that she should avoid conflicts and consciously try to overlook her delusional convictions. She had followed this advice, and seemingly to a great extent had succeeded in "encapsulating" her psychotic ideas.

No. 16428. Male, born 1893, had been psychotic for seven years, when he was admitted to Gaustad Hospital in 1947. When re-examined in 1959, he was classified as a paranoid schizophrenic. Since discharge he had earned the wages of a skilled worker in house building. He lived in a hostel where most inmates were socially destitute persons.

3. OCCUPATION

Our clinical sample is too small for such studies of the influence of occupational status, which *Ödegård* and others have carried out on the basis of official statistics (5, 29, 134, 135).

We have limited our study to the effects of illness upon occupational status. The results are presented in Table 26 (see table).

TABLE 26

OCCUPATION AT RE-EXAMINATION

Occupation at Re-examination	Chronic Schizophrenics in Gaustad Hospital	Chronic Schizophrenics Outside Hospitals	Improved Schizophrenics	Recovered Schizophrenics	Manic-depressive Psychoses	Reactive Psychoses	Total
Advancement	Excluded	2	5	20	5	7	39
Stationary level	Excluded	24	51	69	42	83	269
Decline	Excluded	49	30	7	14	29	129
Total	Excluded	75	86	96	61	119	437

It is remarkable that as many as twenty-six chronic schizophrenics had no decline in occupational status. The improved schizophrenics maintained their occupational level nearly as well as those with affective psychoses. *Harris et al* found in their follow-up study that a comparison of the occupational status of schizophrenics before admission with that after discharge revealed little difference (62).

The recovered schizoprenics were significantly higher in occupational advancement than the other outcome groups (P < 0.001) and were the only group with a tendency to better occupational status. Probably this group has not been essentially hampered in developing better occupational qualifications. A great proportion of the recovered schizophrenics were young people, who with increasing age have been able to qualify themselves for better occupations.

A typical example of what we have classified as recovered schizophrenics is: No. 15352. Female, born 1918. The patient was treated in Gaustad Hospital in 1942 and re-examined in 1959. Prior to admission she studied law and in 1946 she graduated. Afterwards she married and had one child. Although she had her domestic responsibilities, she had for several years been successfully employed in a government office.

Another example is No. 16036. Female, born 1926. She was treated in the hospital in 1945. When re-examined in 1956 she had recovered completely from her schizophrenic psychosis. The patient felt that she had become positively better adjusted after the psychotic period. Previously she had been very withdrawn, sensitive, and bothered by inferiority feelings. After the psychosis she more easily became acquainted with others and gained more self-confidence. She had educated herself as a librarian and was successfully employed.

Patients with schizophrenic defects had often made attempts to improve their occupational status, but as a rule had difficulties in succeeding. No. 16466. Male, born 1916, may serve as an example. He was treated in the hospital in 1947 and re-examined in 1959. In 1951 he began to study at the Agricultural College and graduated in 1955, with quite good results. When he obtained a position as a teacher, however, he failed completely. This was quite understandable, as he was extremely schizoid and eccentric with affective flattening. His pupils complained that they did not learn anything from his lectures and the patient had to leave his job. When he afterwards found a job in a dairy, he lacked practical sense for applying his theoretical knowledge. Then the patient became a book peddler. But his talent for selling was so small that he could barely exist, although his peronal needs were mainly food and a small room which was very poorly furnished.

4. SOCIAL CLASS

Quite a lot of ecological studies indicate that areas with low social standards have high incidence and prevalence rates of mental disorders (5, 37, 48, 49, 67, 99). Other studies show that occupational groups with low income and prestige have increased psychiatric morbidity (29, 108, 134, 135, 140). In particular high rates of schizophrenia seem to be highly correlated with low economic and social standards (5, 29, 48, 49, 67, 108). The manic-depressive psychoses apparently do not show such correlations, and several authors think that they are relatively more frequent in upper classes than in lower socio-economic strata (5, 29, 92, 166, 168). In European studies there are not such great differences as in the American studies. *Ödegård* for instance, finds considerably less difference between various occupational groups than *Clarc* (29, 134, 135). The very great differences arouse suspicion of methodological pitfalls. It may also be that the effects of social factors upon mental health are greater in America than in the socially rather homogeneous Norwegian population. The study of *Inghe* shows, however, a considerable excess morbidity in male schizophrenics among paupers in the capital of Sweden, where the social structure is similar to that in Norway (69).

The studies of *Hollingshead* and *Redlich* revealed not only that the lower social classes have a higher incidence of schizophrenia than the higher social classes, but patients at the lowest socio-economic level had less chance of being discharged from hospital and had more serious obstacles in rehabilitation (67). *Phillips* found that a good prognosis correlated with good social adjustment (143). According to *Brown et al* superior social achievement before admisison was usually significantly related to post hospital success (25). When *Harris et al* compared the social status of schizophrenics with that of their parents, 59 per cent either kept within the same social class or improved upon their parents in this respect (62). According to *Ödegård* the economic status of delayed admissions and their relatives seems to have been somewhat below the average. There were only slight differences between schizophrenics and other functional psychoses (136).

TABLE 27

SOCIAL CLASS BEFORE ADMISSION AND AT RE-EXAMINATION

Social Class Before Admission and at Re-examination	Chronic Schizophrenics in Gaustad Hospital		Chronic Schizophrenics Outside Hospitals		Improved Schizophrenics		Recovered Schizophrenics		Manic-depressive Psychoses		Reactive Psychoses		Total	
	Before adm.	At re-ex.	Before adm.	At re-ex.	Before adm.	At re-ex.	Before adm.	At re-ex.	Before adm.	At re-ex.	Before adm.	At re-ex.	Before adm.	At re-ex.
Above average	6		7	0	9	5	6	5	21	15	7	3	8	4
Average	30		61	36	59	45	72	75	66	71	63	63	57	46
Below average	64		32	49	32	49	22	20	13	8	30	30	35	25
In public care		100		15		1				6		4		25
Total	100	100	100	100	100	100	100	100	100	100	100	100	100	100
No. of cases	118	118	75	75	86	86	96	96	61	61	119	119	555	555

Our comparisons of social class before admission and at re-examination are presented in the table below (see Table 27).

Housewives have been coded in the same class as their husbands, and young persons living at home in the same class as their parents. In the group "above average" we have few patients. These groups include proprietors of business, merchants, factory owners, members of academic professions, etc., who as a rule have higher occupational prestige and better economy than average. In the under average we have all who definitely lie below average standards. Basic criteria are receipt of poor relief or very bad economy related to poor working capacity or alcoholic abuse. For some patients also very poor housing conditions have been a factor for classifying them as below average. This group comprises such occupational groups as unskilled labor and domestic servants. At re-examination patients commited to public care as insane are put in a separate group.

It is seen from the above that our classification builds upon total information from case histories and re-examination interviews. We are well aware that our more "clinical judgment" of social class has not such a numerical exactness, as, for instance, that of the social classification of *Hollingshead* and *Redlich* (67). We know each of our patients and their surroundings quite well. As the same principle of classification is used for all groups, comparisons for various clinical outcome groups should be reliable.

Before admission the manic-depressive group had fewer persons in the below average group than the other outcome groups (P < 0.001). This corresponds well with the previously mentioned social psychiatric studies. On the other hand the chronic schizophrenics in Gaustad Hospital predominantly belonged to the group below average. Compared with the other outcome groups, the proportion of patients below average was significantly greater (P < 0.001). The other schizophrenic outcome groups do not differ much from each other or from the reactive psychoses. These findings may indicate that in the lowest social class it is particularly difficult to adapt outside a mental hospital after having developed a schizophrenic psychosis. Another explanation may be that the low social status of the hospitalized schizophrenics is mainly due to prepsychotic character changes of long duration, preventing them from succeeding in social adaptation at any time of life. Their staying in hospital may also be more related to a serious clinical course of illness than to social factors. As seen later in this chapter, they are also characterized by much more aggressive behavior than the chronic schizophrenics outside mental hospitals. Furthermore, several had been given a trial outside hospitals, but had to be re-admitted because of very uncontrolled behavior.

The most likely explanation is that the chronic hospital group, because of the severe course of illness, belongs predominantly to a low social class and, with their defects, can only with difficulty adapt outside a mental hospital. Clinically the chronic schizophrenics outside mental hospitals had also predominantly slight schizophrenic deterioration, whereas a great percentage of those in the hospital were severely deteriorated.

At re-examination the recovered schizophrenics and the manic-depressives have practically the same social status as before admission. It is remarkable that as many as twenty-seven of the chronic schizophrenics outside mental hospitals are classified in the average group. The improved schizophrenics had before admission practically the same social structure as the reactive psychoses, and at re-examination their proportion below average was only slightly greater than in the reactive psychoses (P < 0.05). This would indicate that slight residuals of a schizophrenic psychosis do not essentially hamper social adaption more than residuals after reactive disorders.

> An example of a well-adapted patient with slight schizophrenic residuals is No. 15133. Male, born 1920. Between 1941 and 1950 he was treated four times in Gaustad Hospital for a periodic catatonia, and he was re-examined in 1956. After discharge he learned to be a turner. This work suited him well, as precision was important and no high speed was required. He saved up money for a new apartment, which was orderly and well equipped. The patient was stiff in movements and facial expression, slightly emotionally blunted and presented a general psychic lameness. He realized that he was very schizoid and related that he had taken an extra job as a book seller in order to counteract

his tendency to seclusion. With the same purpose he regularly invited friends to his flat, especially to Sunday dinner.

Even more remarkable is how No. 17093, male born 1906, maintained his social position. He was treated in Gaustad Hospital in 1949 and 1952 and re-examined in his home in 1956. Then he complained about voices accusing him of adultery and calling him a louse and a communist. He was also influenced by electrical currents acting upon his back and genital organs. Futhermore, he had visual and gustatory hallucinations. He believed that he was controlled by a certain organization and suffered very much from his hallucinations. Nevertheless he had succeeded in leading and enlarging his own firm. Following the advice of the hospital doctors, he never spoke to anybody about his psychotic experiences. He married in 1952, and there was a child of the marriage. He was very fond of his child and lived on good terms with his wife in a modern and well-equipped flat. His wife considered their marriage quite happy. She was well aware of his hallucinatory experiences, but never took up a discussion on this topic. We feel that in this case the attitudes of the patient as well as his wife favored an "encapsulation" of psychotic experiences, contributing to the good social adaptation.

The more common retrogression of social position is illustrated by the following case. No. 14938. Female, born 1901. She was treated in Gaustad Hospital from 1940 to 1953 and re-examined in 1959. The clinical condition was that of an affect-laden paraphrenia. Since discharge the patient had mostly lived with her relatives, and slept during some years in the bathroom of a married sister. She had a university education and prior to admission worked as a pharmacist. After discharge she worked a few hours each day as a domestic servant. Her income was small, and she was in need for some kind of public assistance. But she had small personal needs and took pride in supporting herself. She had also an aversion to doctors. She would not even consult a doctor for an open leg ulcer and was not interested in any help from the hospital.

5. HOUSING CONDITIONS

Several ecological studies reveal that slum areas with poor housing conditions have high rates of mental disorders (5, 49, 67).

Faris found that the average rent paid was considerably higher for manic-depressive psychoses than for schizophrenias (48). *Schroeder* reported that the rates of psychoses were positively correlated with vacant dwelling units, proportion of rental units and houses unfit for use and negatively correlated with average rent paid, dwellings in good condition and home ownership (157).

Previous work on the effect of housing conditions on outcome in functional psychoses is scanty. *Brown* and co-workers found that chronic mental patients after discharge from a hospital often succeeded, when they lived in lodgings (25).

We assume that the housing conditions can, to a great extent, be considered as a measure of social standard. Those living in lodgings and hostels may also be considered as a socially isolated group. The problems of social isolation will be dealt with further in other parts of this chapter. The results of our investigations are presented in the following table (see Table 28).

As for social class, housewives and children living at home have been coded in the same group as the family supporter. Thus living in his own house or farm does not imply that the patient is himself in posession of the farm or his own house. The distinctions between good and poor apartments are not always clear-cut. There are hardly any typical slum districts in Norway, and we have defined as poor apartments such dwellings which were decidedly below average standards. Such factors as overcrowding, old houses and neglected repair were taken into consideration.

In the group "rooming with others" we have included lodgings, hostels, institutions or nursing homes (the latter category mainly at re-examination). In general the three first groups have good and the last two groups have poor housing conditions.

Before admission the manic-depressives had the greatest proportion with their own farm or houses. Compared with the other outcome groups this feature was statistically significant at the 0.001 level. Poor housing conditions were in, particular common, for the chronic schizophrenics in Gaustad Hospital. A greater proportion than in any other group was coded as living in poor apartments (P < 0.001). The chronic schizophrenics outside mental hospitals had practically the same housing conditions as the improved schizophrenics. Compared with the other schizo-

TABLE 28

Housing Conditions Before Admission and at Re-examination

Housing Conditions Before Admission and at Re-examination	Chronic Schizophrenics in Gaustad Hospital		Chronic Schizophrenics Outside Hospitals		Improved Schizophrenics		Recovered Schizophrenics		Manic-depressive Psychoses		Reactive Psychoses		Total	
	Before adm.	At re-ex.	Before adm.	At re-ex.	Before adm.	At re-ex.	Before adm.	At re-ex.	Before adm.	At re-ex.	Before adm.	At re-ex.	Before adm.	At re-ex.
Farm	19		11	8	12	8	8	10	15	13	8	8	12	9
Own house	5		15	12	16	13	9	25	31	33	23	28	15	22
Good apartment	13		27	21	27	27	57	50	26	28	24	29	28	32
Poor apartment	36		18	18	12	13	7	5	8	0	21	11	19	10
Rooming with others, lodgings, hostels etc.	27		29	41	33	39	19	10	20	26	24	24	26	27
Total	100		100	100	100	100	100	100	100	100	100	100	100	100
No. of cases	118		75	75	86	86	96	96	61	61	119	119	555	437

phrenic outcome groups the recovered schizophrenics had significantly fewer persons in poor apartments or "rooming with others" (P < 0.001). This difference is mainly due to the poor housing conditions of the chronic schizophrenics staying in the hospital, but even for the remaining statistically significant at the 0.001 level.

In the group "rooming with others" the improved schizophrenics (33%) had the greatest and the recovered schizophrenics (19%) the smallest percentage.

At *re-examination* the affective psychoses had practically the same housing conditions as before admission. The recovered schizophrenics had better housing conditions than before admission. No marked worsening of housing conditions could be established for improved schizophrenics and chronic schizophrenics living outside mental hospitals. But in these categories the percentages of persons rooming with others increased to 40 per cent, whereas the recovered schizophrenic only had 10 per cent.

We can conclude that before admission the manic-depressives had the best housing conditions, and recovered schizophrenics were considerably better off than the other schizophrenic groups. At re-examination the housing conditions were little changed for unhospitalized cases, except for some better standards in recovered schizophrenics. Several in the latter group were young people who obtained better housing conditions with increasing age.

We could give several examples of extremely bad housing conditions for patients with schizophrenic defects. No. 14967. Female, born 1915, was treated in the hospital in 1940 and re-examined in 1956. The patient had broken all connections with relatives and was not found in the local population registers. After much inquiry we found that she lived in a hostel in Oslo for nearly two years. She slept in a great dormitory together with twenty other women. This patient suffered very much from hallucinations. Voices accused her of adultery, and she felt that men came into her bed in the night and raped her. As she had never had sexual relations with men, this annoyed her very much. She recounted her hallucinatory experiences with such indecent expressions, that even socially destitute "half-prostitutes" in the dormitory considered her speech too crude. All, however, were aware that the patient was insane. They pitied her and tried to overlook her behavior, although she often wandered about the whole night complaining about sexual abuse. The patient was very angry with the doctors in the hospital and protested violently against a proposal of treatment. But six months later the situation was so intolerable, that a compulsory admission was unavoidable. When she came to the hospital a considerable amount of money was found in her clothes, showing that she could have afforded better housing conditions. She was furious with the doctors, saying that they raped her, would murder her and take her money. With chlorpromazine she improved considerably. The patient had worked as a domestic servant, and her employers could report that she was exceptionally efficient. One of them let her have a room in her flat, to which the patient was discharged in 1957. After discharge the patient continued with chlorpromazine. We had contact with her from time to time, the last time in the summer of 1959. She still had her hallucinations, but suffered less and was thankful for what the hospital had done for her.

Another example is No. 16503. Male, born 1921. He was treated in the hospital in 1947 and 1955 and re-examined in 1959. After discharge he wandered about and had no domicile. After much search we found him in a tent in the woods outside Oslo, where he stayed during summer. In the winter he slept on staircases, and when he had money in hostels. He considered it too expensive to have a room of his own. But he had been able to support himself by casual unskilled work. His appearance was emaciated, and his clothes disorderly. His speech was confused and he related bizarre religious and philosophical speculations. He was very dissatisfied with his stay in the hospital, and thought he had been treated like an animal against his will.

No. 16835. Female, born 1917, was treated in the hospital in 1948. When re-examined in 1956, she presented a mild schizophrenic deterioration. She lived in a small room measuring 2 x 3 m. The window was covered with wrapping paper, and she slept on an iron bed covered with rags. The room was unbelievably dirty and disorderly.

6. MIGRATION

Ödegård has shown that emigrants from Norway to Minnesota had a considerable excess psychiatric morbidity compared with the population of Norway and native-born Americans (124). Within Norway as a rule migrant groups have less insanity than the non-migrant. The main exception is a high rate in migrants to Oslo, by far the largest town in Norway (126, 138). There seems to be fair agreement that migration is an important factor for the incidence of mental illness (99, 109). But in prognostic studies the factor of migration has previously not been analyzed.

With our comparatively small sample, the analysis has been limited to four migrational groups. We assumed that just as rates are differently related to migrational factors, so might prognosis be. Furthermore, the migrations of patients after discharge might indirectly throw some light upon tendencies of various clinical groups to drift away from their residences at birth. The migrants are probably more socially isolated than those staying at home. This may particularly be so in the case of those moving to Oslo. So the analysis of migration can contribute to the elucidation of the problems of social isolation. The results of our investigations are presented in the table below (see Table 29).

As in the statistical studies of *Ödegård* and *Astrup* on migration, we have before admission compared the community of birth and community of residence at hospital admission (138) respectively at re-examination.

The proportion of the patients who were classified as migrants at the time of first admission varies from one outcome group to another, but there is no consistent association between pre-psychotic mobility and prognosis. Migrants are common in manic-depressive (49 per cent) as well as in chronic schizophrenic hospital patients (48 per cent). The difference in age on admission may explain the unexpected similarity between these two groups: the manic-depressives will have been exposed to the possibility of migration for a longer time. As to the chronic schizophrenics their migrant status may actually have made discharge from the hospital more difficult.

Low proportions of migrants (35 per cent) are found in recovered schizophrenics and in reactive psychoses, but the percentage is nearly as low in the poor-outcome group of chronic schizophrenics, and the association between spatial mobility and poor prognosis is far from clear.

TABLE 29

MIGRATION BEFORE ADMISSION AND AT RE-EXAMINATION

Migration Before Admission and at Re-examination	Chronic Schizophrenics in Gaustad Hospital	Chronic Schizophrenics Outside Hospitals		Improved Schizophrenics		Recovered Schizophrenics		Manic-depressive Psychoses		Reactive Psychoses		Total	
	At re-ex.	Before adm.	At re-ex.	Before adm.	At re-ex.	Before adm.	At re-ex.	Before adm.	At re-ex.	Before adm.	At re-ex.	Before adm.	At re-ex.
Non-migrant	52	61	59	55	37	65	57	51	51	65	62	58	54
Migrants to Oslo	7	17	28	22	35	12	25	18	23	14	25	14	27
Migrants from Oslo	2	3	4	0	2	1	0	0	3	2	0	1	2
Other migrants	39	19	9	23	26	22	18	31	23	19	13	27	17
Total	100	100	100	100	100	100	100	100	100	100	100	100	100
No. of cases	118	75	75	86	86	96	96	61	61	119	119	555	437

At the time of re-examination the pattern has changed somewhat, in that the "migrants to Oslo" group has increased at the
expense of the other types of migrants. Most likely the location of
the hospital in Oslo is responsible for this. Many patients prefer
to stay in Oslo after discharge, in spite of the hospital policy
recommending them to return home. In some cases the possibility
of continued contact with the hospital may be the reason, in
others a desire to disappear in the crowd rather than to face the
old and familiar environment.

The greatest increase in spatial mobility is seen in the improved schizophrenic group: from 45 to 63 per cent of the migrants (significant at the 0.001 per cent level). This is probably
a direct result of the adjustment problems which these patients
meet after discharge.

It may be concluded that migrant or non-migrant status
previous to first admission does not seem to be associated with
outcome, and has no predictive value. After discharge increased
spatial mobility occurs, particularly in improved schizophrenics,
as a consequence of social maladjustment. Also there is a tendency
for discharged patients to move to Oslo.

As an example of the improved schizophrenic migrants to
Oslo, we would mention No. 16296. Male, born 1918 and treated
in the hospital in 1946. After much inquiry we received information about where he lived, but more than ten visits had to be
made until he was found in 1956. He lived in a small waggon
with 3 square meters of floor. There was only room for a bed
and a chair, and everything was as dirty as possible. Previously
his waggon had served the combined functions of a sleeping room
and a "shop" for selling hot dogs. But the health authorities
did not find his "shop" sufficiently hygienic for selling food. Then
he found work as a messenger. The patient related that he traveled
much around the country during the first years after discharge
and then moved to the outskirts of Oslo. He stressed that he
systematically had moved nearer to the center of the town, where
he liked best to be. Now he had placed his waggon in the back
yard of a house in the East End. He did not have permission to do
so, but he told us that the house owner who was a Jew and a hu-
mane person did not object to his taking up a temporary residence
there during his migration towards the center of the town. The

patient led a lonely life without intimate connections with any people.

Another example is No. 14837. Male, born 1913. He was treated in Gaustad Hospital in 1939 and re-examined in 1956. Since 1948 he had been in Oslo. He lived in a hostel where he shared a room with two others. Like the former case he worked as a messenger. He was embittered because he thought the hospital stay had branded him as a criminal. Prior to admission he was married, but his wife demanded a divorce a few years before he went to Oslo. The patient thought that Oslo was most peaceful. He had no contacts with his family and led a lonely life, with horseracing his only interest.

An example of the non-schizophrenic migrants to Oslo is No. 16910. Male, born 1905, treated in the hospital in 1949. When re-examined in 1959 the hospital diagnosis of reactive psychosis could be catamnestically verified. His psychosis was precipitated by marital conflicts because of infidelity on the part of his wife. After discharge he divorced her and lived the first years at home in a small industrial community, but he felt uncomfortable as everybody knew about his mental illness. He liked much better to be in Oslo where nobody cared about his personal affairs and where he had many acquaintances and also a girl friend. After the experiences of his marriage, however, he hesitated to remarry.

7. MARITAL STATUS

From all statistics it appears that the single have higher rates of insanity than the married. The widowed, and especially the divorced also had higher rates than the married (34, 72, 123, 127, 132, 133, 145, 160, 163). There is every reason to assume that the married represent a biologically and socially favorable selection. Several authors have found that married status is prognostically favorable in functional psychoses (122, 156). In particular there is agreement that this is a favorable factor in schizophrenia (15, 72, 141, 143, 156, 171).

The following table shows the marital status at admission for the total material (see Table 30).

The table reveals that the manic-depressives have less single

TABLE 30

MARITAL STATUS IN TOTAL MATERIAL BEFORE ADMISSION

| Outcome | Marital Status Before Admission | | |
	Single	Married, Divorced or Widowed	Total
Deteriorated schizophrenics	304	112	416
Improved schizophrenics	87	30	117
Recovered schizophrenics	79	52	131
Reactive psychoses	94	112	206
Manic-depressive psychoses	35	67	102
Total	599	373	972

persons than the reactive psychoses, but the differences are not great. The two affective groups have, however, considerably less single persons than the schizophrenic groups. Again there were less recovered than improved and deteriorated schizophrenics with single status. We can thus confirm the unfavorable prognostic importance of single marital status referred to in the literature. If corrected for age on the basis of the 1946 population census, the observed married persons would for the five outcome groups make out the following percentages of the expected married: deteriorated schizophrenics 49 per cent, improved schizophrenics 48 per cent, recovered schizophrenics 75 per cent, reactive psychoses 85 per cent, and manic-depressive psychoses 88 per cent. The next step was to present the more detailed comparisons in personally seen patients (see Table 31).

Before admission the manic-depressives had less single persons than the other outcome groups. The reactive psychoses lay midway between the manic-depressives and the schizophrenics. Recovered schizophrenics had a considerably lower proportion of single persons than the other schizophrenic outcome groups. There were so few divorced, separated and re-married persons before admission that no conclusions could be drawn about these marital groups.

After hospital admission very few of the chronic and im-

TABLE 31

MARITAL STATUS BEFORE ADMISSION AND AT RE-EXAMINATION

Marital Status Before Admission and at Re-examination	Chronic Schizophrenics in Gaustad Hospital		Chronic Schizophrenics Outside Hospitals		Improved Schizophrenics		Recovered Schizophrenics		Manic-depressive Psychoses		Reactive Psychoses		Total	
	Before adm.	At re-ex.	Before adm.	At re-ex.	Before adm.	At re-ex.	Before adm.	At re-ex.	Before adm.	At re-ex.	Before adm.	At re-ex.	Before adm.	At re-ex.
Single	76	73	68	61	71	61	58	24	34	28	41	29	59	47
Married	14	9	29	20	25	26	40	64	49	41	53	49	34	34
Widowed	6	8	1	4	2	3	0	1	11	21	3	6	4	6
Divorced or separated	2	9	2	15	2	9	2	9	2	7	3	14	2	11
Remarried	2	1	0	0	0	1	0	2	4	3	0	2	1	2
Total	100	100	100	100	100	100	100	100	100	100	100	100	100	100
No. of cases	118	118	75	75	86	86	96	96	61	61	119	119	555	555

proved schizophrenics married. Also few of the manic-depressives have married. But they belong to higher age groups and have still a small proportion of single persons, quite similar to that of the reactive psychoses. With respect to single status the difference between improved and chronic schizophrenics on one hand and recovered schizophrenics on the other hand was even greater than before admission.

The widowed were found particularly among the manic-depressives. The reactive psychoses, with 14 per cent, had a great proportion of divorced or separated.

Our study shows that those with schizophrenic defects fail more in the ability to obtain marital status than to keep working capacity, social position and housing conditions.

When considering the individual cases there have been many problems connected with marriage. An example of the divorced patients with reactive psychosis is No. 16774. Female, born 1919. In her personality structure she was immature and sensitive with hysterical traits, she had been engaged, but her friend died. In 1946 she married a man who was nervous and an alcoholic. They lived in a very poor apartment in barracks which had been used by German soldiers during the war. When the husband was drinking, he was brutal and brought other women into the room. During the years 1946-48 the patient had three criminal abortions, strongly encouraged by her husband. In 1948 she was admitted to Gaustad Hospital for a reactive depression with hypochondriacal delusions. Her husband disappeared, and when the patient was reexamined in 1957, she had been divorced for a year. She had several psychosomatic complaints, such as headache, lumbago and cardiac neurosis. In 1959 the patient was again seen. Now she was considerably better, had re-married in spite of the previous martial experiences, but this time with a religious man who did not use alcohol.

No. 16950. Female, born 1914, had married a man twenty-six years older than herself, who had pulmonary tuberculosis and was unable to work. They had four children and lived very poorly. The patient was frigid and gradually developed disgust towards her husband who always would pet her and was very demanding sexually. In 1949 she had a sexual escapade with another man.

Shortly afterwards she became depressed, made an attempt at suicide and was admitted to Gaustad Hospital. When re-examined in 1957, she related that she had divorced and remarried in 1953, In her second marriage she had stabilized but suffered to a considerable degree from neurasthenic symptoms.

Several persons had married after discharge without telling their spouses about their mental illness. No. 15101. Male, born 1923 was treated in the hospital in 1941 and re-examined in 1959. When he was met at home together with his wife, it was quite an embarrassing situation. The patient feared very much that his wife would get to know that he had been treated in a mental hospital. Nothing was mentioned about it to her.
Another example is No. 15677. Female, born 1919. She was treated in the hospital in 1944 and 1954. In 1945 she became engaged and was soon pregnant. Her mother then told her fiancé about the mental illness. The engagement was broken and an abortion was carried out on medical indications. In 1948 the patient became acquainted with her later husband through an advertisement. This time the patient also became pregnant, but her mother would not interfere again, and the patient married and bore her child. Shortly after the birth she had a period of persecutory delusions, and the family told the husband about her disease. When she became pregnant the third time in 1953, an abortion was carried out jointly with sterilization. In 1956 the patient was re-examined. She was extremely suspicious and had periodical auditory hallucinations. Her husband had to be very careful in order to avoid irritating her during the hallucinated periods. But he praised his wife for keeping the house in good order, and in spite of her illness they lived happily together. After the re-examination the patient several times consulted the examiner in order to obtain help for reduction of taxes because of her illness.

For several patients, marriage seemed to favor a mental stabilization. An example is No. 16459. Male, born 1919. He was treated in the hospital in 1947 and re-examined in 1956. The first months after discharge he would not leave his home, and was haunted by fears of being homosexual. His brother induced him to seek more contact with other people. In 1951 he married. His marriage was happy, and he thought that his wife had helped him to get out of the crisis of his youth. He took up a profession as an artist and earned a good reputation. Clinically the patient could be classified as a recovered schizophrenic.

No. 15991. Male, born 1916. His first admission to Gaustad Hospital occurred in 1945 in relation to a love affair with a married woman. After discharge he married her, but their marriage was full of conflicts. He had a second psychotic period in 1951 and was then divorced. When re-examined in 1956 he related that he had remarried in 1954 and had a daughter. He felt that his second marriage had made it possible for him to become mentally stable and to advance in his occupational status. Clinically the patient was classified as a recovered schizophrenic.

8. CHILDREN

Several authors have shown that the fertility of the insane is smaller than that of the general population (33, 44, 72, 121). Manic-depressives do not lie much under the average. But the schizophrenics have on the whole very few children. The main reason for this is apparently that the marriage rate is considerably smaller than for the general population. In a similar way as with marriage we thought that an ability to beget children might be considered as a sign of favorable social adaptation before as well as after admission. The results of our investigations are presented below (see Table 32).

Before admission the recovered schizophrenics had only slightly more children than those with schizophrenic defects (not significant). The chronic schizophrenics outside mental hospitals had even the same percentage without children as the recovered schizophrenics (69%). But only 20 per cent of the chronic schizophrenics in Gaustad Hospital had children. Patients with affective psychoses showed significantly greater tendency than the schizophrenics to have children (P < 0.001), but only in the manic-depressive group the majority have children.

After discharge eighty-three patients had children. Only six of the manic-depressives had more children. This is mainly related to their belonging to higher age groups, but our clinical interviews indicate that several also have avoided having more children because of the risk that the children might inherit their disease. The recovered schizophrenics and those with reactive

TABLE 32

CHILDREN BEFORE ADMISSION AND AT RE-EXAMINATION

Children Before Admission and at Re-examination (After Admission)	Chronic Schizophrenics in Gaustad Hospital		Chronic Schizophrenics Outside Hospitals		Improved Schizophrenics		Recovered Schizophrenics		Manic-depressive Psychoses		Reactive Psychoses		Total	
	Before adm.	At re-ex.	Before adm.	At re-ex.	Before adm.	At re-ex.	Before adm.	At re-ex.	Before adm.	At re-ex.	Before adm.	At re-ex.	Before adm.	At re-ex.
No children	80	96	69	93	76	90	69	65	43	90	51	80	66	85
Children	20	4	31	7	24	10	31	35	57	10	49	20	34	15
Total	100	100	100	100	100	100	100	100	100	100	100	100	100	100
No. of cases	118	118	75	75	86	86	96	96	61	61	119	119	555	555

psychoses had, compared with the others, a significantly greater proportion with children (P < 0.001). Among recovered schizophrenics even more had had children after admisison than before admission. From a genetic point of view this may be problematic, as such patients, as seen in Chapter VI, have many schizophrenic relatives. On the other hand the tendency to marry, have children, succeed in work, and improve profession and housing conditions, may also indicate that the recovered schizophrenics, in most aspects, are very well socially adapted.

In our material there are very few illegitimate children. *Ödegård* has calculated that the married psychotics had practically the same fertility as the married in the general population.

Fifteen per cent of the patients had had children after discharge from the hospital, and we have seen several tragic examples.

No. 15206. Male, born 1915. Was admitted to Gaustad Hospital in 1942 and 1946 for paranoid schizophrenia and had a good remission. In 1947 he married and had two children born in 1949 and 1952. After his third psychotic attack in 1953, he has been continually in the hospital. In his family there was a considerable genetic loading of psychoses and his wife feared very much to beget more children. When visiting his wife the patient was sexually demanding, and he refused sterilization, which was wanted by his wife and recommended by the doctors. Another complication preventing discharge was that the patient disturbed the work on the family's farm with all kinds of senseless "technical improvements."

No. 16784. Female, born 1929, was treated in Gaustad Hospital in 1948 for catatonic schizophrenia. After discharge she married and in 1952 and 1955 had two children. There were many psychoses in her family, and during her last pregnancy she was so nervous that an abortion was medically recommended. Shortly after the birth she was re-admitted to Gaustad Hospital where she stayed until 1957. Against the advice of the hospital she was taken out of the hospital by her mother. After a few months the patient was brought to the hospital with a catatonic excitation. While she was out of the hospital she lived together with another man. Her husband wanted a divorce in 1956, and in 1959 we received information that the patient was divorced.

No. 16943. Male, born 1921. There was a considerable genetic loading of psychoses in his family. He married in 1947 and had two children in 1951 and 1956. In 1949 he was treated in Gaustad Hospital for paranoid schizophrenia. From 1957 to 1959 he had to be admitted three times to the hospital. His elder child was very nervous and his wife became so later. She had a complete nervous breakdown in 1958 and wrote to her husband that she could not endure living with him unless he should recover completely from his psychosis. She took a job in order to support herself and her children. After this the patient was discharged to his parental family, but was soon readmitted. The patient was considered to have been a deteriorated schizophrenic for some years and obviously had minimal chances of recovery.

No. 16333. Male, born 1921, was treated in Gaustad Hospital from 1946 to 1954 and discharged as insane with the diagnosis of schizophrenia. When re-examined in1959 he presented a clinical picture typical of eccentric hebephrenia. He had married in 1956 and had three children ranging from three years to three months. His wife was a fat feebleminded woman, who was well content with her husband. The patient had become psychotic during service with the Norwegian Forces in England in World War II. He, therefore, received a veteran's pension and one of his relatives helped him get a job. Thus he had been able to obtain a good flat and to support his family.

No. 15103. Male, born 1904, was treated in Gaustad Hospital in 1941 for paranoid schizophrenia. He married in 1945 and had a son. His working ability was so reduced that he could not support his family, but he was so emotionally blunted that he did not bother about this.

No. 15446. Female, born 1920 was treated in Gaustad Hospital for a manic-depressive psychosis in 1942. She married in 1944 and had two children. In 1946 she was sterilized. After their marriage her husband became psychotic and developed a schizophrenic deterioration. The patient had several psychotic periods and when she was re-examined in 1957 she was so mentally unstable that she could not take care of her children.

No. 15678. Female, born 1924 was treated in Gaustad Hospital in 1944 under the diagnosis of schizophrenia. Prior to admission she had been very promiscuous and had sexual relations with several German occupation soldiers. In the hospital sterilization was recommended, but she refused. In 1959 the patient was re-examined in her home. She did not reveal any symptoms of schizophrenic defect, but was very neurotic. She related that she had married in 1951 and had a son of five years. As her marriage was very unhappy, she divorced her husband, an alcoholic who could not support his child. In 1960 the patient consulted the examiner in order to receive a medical certificate because she was too nervous to work. An important reason contributing to this was that her son was so nervous that he could not go to the kindergarten. The patient felt that her son was the only thing which made her life worth living. It is possible, however, that the proposed sterilization would have been the best solution.

9. SEXUAL LIFE

As shown in Chapter IV schizophrenics with a poor prognosis have very often schizoid personality traits. A schizoid personality is probably a marriage handicap as well as a hindrance to the ability to obtain sexual contacts.

For the above-mentioned reasons it sounds probable that information about sexual life may be of prognostic value. *Phillips* found that a good prognosis correlated with a good recent sexual adjustment (143). *Wirt* and *Simon* thought that patients with poor prognosis had poor heterosexual relationships throughout life, no interest in girls or fear of girls (171). Our findings are presented in the table below (see Table 33).

Under the term "long-lasting sexual relations," we have coded patients who have been married or engaged or have had sexual relations for at least one year with the same person. Others with sexual experience are coded in the group with "sporadic sexual relations." The group with "no known sexual experiences" includes a few cases in which we were not able to obtain certain information. This applies, however, rather equally to all outcome groups.

Before admission especially the manic-depressives have been able to obtain long-lasting sexual relations (76%). Then follow the reactive psychoses (64%) and the recovered schizophrenics (55%).

TABLE 33

SEXUAL LIFE BEFORE ADMISSION AND AT RE-EXAMINATION

Sexual Life Before Admission and at Re-examination (After Admission)	Chronic Schizophrenics in Gaustad Hospital		Chronic Schizophrenics Outside Hospitals		Improved Schizophrenics		Recovered Schizophrenics		Manic-depressive Psychoses		Reactive Psychoses		Total	
	Before adm.	At re-ex.	Before adm.	At re-ex.	Before adm.	At re-ex.	Before adm.	At re-ex.	Before adm.	At re-ex.	Before adm.	At re-ex.	Before adm.	At re-ex.
No known sexual experiences	48	87	50	67	43	55	29	21	22	40	24	31	36	51
Sporadic sexual relations	16	3	9	8	20	8	16	3	2	2	12	8	13	5
Long lasting sexual relations	36	10	41	25	37	37	55	76	76	58	64	61	51	44
Total	100	100	100	100	100	100	100	100	100	100	100	100	100	100
No. of cases	118	118	75	75	86	86	96	96	61	61	119	119	555	555

The improved and two chronic schizophrenic groups do not differ much from each other with regard to sexual experiences. But they have considerably more with no known sexual experiences than the recovered schizophrenics (P < 0.01). Among those with long-lasting sexual relations 11 per cent of the affective and 39 per cent of the schizophrenic psychoses had single marital status. After admission the sexual activity has for obvious reasons been smallest for the chronic schizophrenics in Gaustad Hospital (76 of them have been discharged for some periods). But also the chronic and improved schizophrenics outside mental hospitals have a considerably greater proportion with no sexual experiences than the recovered schizophrenics (P < 0.001), and the differences are even greater than before admission. The recovered schizophrenics have in fact the greatest proportion of longstanding sexual relations after discharge from hospital with 76 per cent, then follow the reactive psychoses with 61 per cent and the manic-depressives with 58 per cent, but the manic-depressive group includes many older widowed persons.

We can conclude that an ability to obtain long-lasting sexual relations is prognostically favorable, before as well as after admission.

Although the deteriorated schizophrenics as a rule showed little sexual activity after discharge, there were several exceptions. No. 15828. Female, born 1922 was first admitted to Gaustad Hospital in 1944. After discharge she had a very unstable work record and led a promiscuous sexual life. In 1950 she became pregnant and an abortion was carried out on medical indications. When she became pregnant the second time in 1954, she bore a child, but was completely unable to care for it. She was placed in public care at a farm as insane in 1956. As she often went away, lingering about with men, she was readmitted to the hospital. Here she was sterilized in 1958. The sterilization certainly ought to have been performed in 1950.

Another example is No. 13. Female, born 1890. The patient was admitted to the hospital in 1950 and re-examined in 1959. Prior to admission she had been psychotic for fourteen years, and was single. From 1954 to 1956 she was married to an elderly gentleman of over seventy years, who was an alcoholic and existed by poor relief. They had divorced and the patient related that she had several lovers. Together with a forty-four year old sailor she enjoyed sexual intercourse as if she was a girl in her twenties. A neighbor could confirm that the patient was often visited by men. She was considered by everybody as insane. She would urinate in the middle of the road without caring about people seeing her, and was completely uninhibited.

The sexual adjustment of married schizophrenics was often poor. No. 16153. Male, born 1913, was treated in the hospital for paranoid schizophrenia in 1945. He was married prior to admission and had two children, born 1941 and 1946. In 1956 he was re-examined in his home. As his opinion about sexual life he stated that when one has had sexual intercourse approximately 3000 times with one's wife, one gets bored with it. His wife explained tearfully that although he was jealous and brutal, she kept the home together. In 1958 he was readmitted to the hospital and revealed fantastic ideas of jealousy. After treatment with ataraxic drugs he could be discharged to his wife who now was very content with him.

Patients with non-schizophrenic course of illness often stabilized in sexual life with the years. No. 16563. Female, born 1927, was the daughter of a lay preacher and strictly brought up to a moral life. When she left her home and came to Oslo, she started to keep late hours and was sexually promiscuous. After a car trip with a girl and two boy friends, when sexual intercourse took place during the drive, the patient became psychotic the following day. When admitted to Gaustad Hospital she presented schizophrenic symptoms. After discharge she returned to her home, where she took part in religious life and became engaged to a man who was accepted by her family. As she became pregnant, an illegal abortion was performed, and she broke her engagement. Afterwards she developed religious scruples, became depressed, and sought voluntary admission to Gaustad Hospital. In 1956 she was re-examined in her home in Oslo. She had recovered completely from the psychosis, was happily married and felt that she had matured with the years.

10. CONTACTS WITH RELATIVES

Characteristic of schizophrenic deterioration is the loss of emotional contact with other people and, in particular, close relatives. Their tendency to autism and loneliness is agreed. Several authors have assumed on one hand that human isolation is predisposing for schizophrenia, and on the other hand that schizophrenics avoid contact with others because they are too hypersensitive to tolerate intimate emotional relationships. The reports about high rates of insanity in emigrants, refugees or other minority groups may indicate that social isolation is of significance for high incidences of insanity (38, 84, 109, 124, 172). Some ecological studies also point in the same direction, and *Faris* as early as 1934 provided data favoring a hypothesis of cultural isolation being related to the schizophrenic personality (47).

In a clinical material the factor of social isolation could probably to some extent be elucidated by contacts with relatives. As a measure for such contacts we have coded those with whom the patients have lived before admission and at re-examination.

From the studies of *Ödegård* it appeared that 62 per cent of delayed admissions lived with relatives, and there were no marked differences between schizophrenics and other diagnostic categories (136). *Brown et al* made the observation that discharged patients more often were readmitted when they went to parents or spouses. Those living alone or with other kin had considerably more success. It was pointed out that perhaps it is not always beneficial for a schizophrenic to return to the close emotional ties of a parental or marital household (25).

The results of our investigation are presented in the following table (see Table 34).

Before admisison we have taken the social surroundings where the patients lived when they were recognized as mentally ill. At re-examination the last known social surroundings for a few hospitalized affective psychoses is coded. For the chronic schizophrenics in Gaustad Hospital we did not code where they lived when discharged. As many as forty-two had been continually in the hospital. Nineteen had been given a trial in public care, and fifty-seven had been discharged to their homes.

Before admission the chronic and improved schizophrenics, to a greater extent than the other outcome groups, lived alone (P < 0.001). Those with schizophrenic defects were also living with parents more than the others (P < 0.001).

TABLE 34

CONTACTS WITH RELATIVES BEFORE ADMISSION AND AT RE-EXAMINATION

Living With Whom Before Admission and at Re-examination	Chronic Schizophrenics in Gaustad Hospital		Chronic Schizophrenics Outside Hospitals		Improved Schizophrenics		Recovered Schizophrenics		Manic-depressive Psychoses		Reactive Psychoses		Total	
	Before adm.	At re-ex.	Before adm.	At re-ex.	Before adm.	At re-ex.	Before adm.	At re-ex.	Before adm.	At re-ex.	Before adm.	At re-ex.	Before adm.	At re-ex.
Parents	42		40	21	40	16	38	10	10	3	22	7	33	11
Spouses	14		29	19	21	26	40	66	51	41	51	52	34	43
Other relatives	8		2	11	2	12	2	4	18	25	11	12	7	11
Alone	36		29	49	37	46	20	20	21	31	16	29	26	35
Total	100		100	100	100	100	100	100	100	100	100	100	100	100
No. of cases	118		75	75	86	86	96	96	61	61	119	119	555	437

At re-examination less patients are living with parents. Considerably more patients live alone than before admission, and the differences were statistically significant at the 0.001 level. Persons living alone had increased from 34 to 48 per cent in those with schizophrenic defects, and from 19 to 26 per cent in the remaining.

Our data show that a lonely life is an unfavorable prognostic factor before admission as well as after discharge.

From a statistical point of view "living with relatives" was favorable, but our patients have certainly often been great burdens on their relatives. No. 56. Male, born 1906 was treated in Gaustad Hospital in 1950 for paranoid schizophrenia and re-examined in 1956. He lived together with his eighty year old mother and a sister. The sister related that the patient had become increasingly brutal. He struck her for the slightest criticism, and she could demonstrate bruises after his beating. The patient used obscene language, and had a habit of opening all windows, even in cold winter. His mother considered him as recovered, only fearing that he might catch a cold because he had not sufficient warm clothes to endure the constant draft. The patient spoke about voices shouting at him. He complained very much about his hospital stay, which he considered as unlawful violence carried out by the police. His sister said that she could no longer endure to have the patient at home, and a re-admission was recommended. Up to 1960 the patient had still remained outside mental hospitals.

No. 16147. Female, born 1914, was treated in the hospital in 1945 and re-examined in 1956. The patient was living with her sister and was incapable of doing any work. She had strong hallucinations and complained about men breaking into the house and raping her. Furthermore, she scratched herself, carried out minor self-mutilations and accused her sister of doing this to her. The patient was very discontented with the hospitalization and was extremely suspicious of doctors. Her sister considered the patient's behavior as a great strain, but would try to care for her as long as possible.

No. 15835. Female, born 1905, was treated in the hospital in

1944 for paranoid schizophrenia. In 1959 she was re-examined in her home. She was very angry because her husband had sent her to the hospital and would have nothing to do with the hospital and its doctors. At admission fantastic ideas of jealousy were outstanding in the clinical picture. During the follow-up interview she related that she suffered from voices uttering unpleasant accusations. Since discharge she had been a great trial to the husband. Often she was so angry that her shouting could be heard far away. In the house she did practically no work, leaving this to her husband, who, because of her dislike of mental hospitals did not venture to arrange a new admission.

No. 15213. Male, born 1916 was treated in Gaustad Hospital in 1942 for catatonic schizophrenia. When re-examined in 1956 he lived with his siblings and mother on the family farm. Since 1952 he had not worked. Most of the time was spent in bed, complaining that his body warmth had vanished. For four years the family had hoped for a recovery, but in connection with the follow-up interview it was decided to have the patient re-admitted. After treatment with ataraxic drugs and ECT he improved considerably. His family was very glad that he could take up the farm work again and did not pay much attention to his somewhat peculiar behavior.

As examples of the lonely lives of patients with schizophrenic defects we present two case histories.

No. 14736. Male, born 1913, was admitted to Gaustad Hospital in 1938 and re-examined in 1957. He lived in the woods in a small cottage of 3 by 3 metres, which he had rented for the whole year, although other people could barely exist there in the summer time. Everything was as dirty and disorderly as it could be. The patient had stereotyped grimaces and mannerisms and during the interview lay masturbating in his bed. Since discharge he had been a vagrant for several years. Now he was content with having a house to himself. His main wish was to live at peace alone. Women had never interested him, and his personal needs were small. Although he only worked during summer, he had saved up a considerable amount of money. In the winter he preferred to stay in his cottage, mainly lying on his bed.

No. 17116. Male, born 1908, was admitted to Gaustad Hospital in 1949 and re-examined in 1956. He had moved around in Oslo and after much inquiry we received the information that he worked on a newspaper from 1 to 5 o'clock in the night. Between those hours he was called up on the telephone and an interview was arranged in the hostel where he lived. In the hostel he was considered as peculiar. Let nobody come into his room and had always drawn the blinds down. The key hole was tightened in order to avoid any observation from outside. When the examiner came into his room, it was noticed that all his food and other belongings were wrapped in paper. The patient explained that he wanted to protect against rays and some mystical kinds of bacteria. He underlined that his physical condition was excellent as he trained keenly, doing much walking and skating. He complained about having lost jobs several times because it became known that he had been treated in Gaustad Hospital. For this reason he avoided contact with other people.

11. ATTITUDE OF RELATIVES TOWARDS PATIENTS

It is a common assumption that conflicts and hostile emotional relationships with relatives play a great role in the causation of mental disorders. Also it sounds likely that attitudes of relatives may be of importance for discharge from hospital and post-hospital adjustment.

Harris et al, however, considered it surprising that relatives pressed for discharge of a large proportion of difficult patients (62). The poor post-hospital adjustment for schizophrenics going to parental groups, as reported by *Brown et al*, might even throw doubt upon the value of positive reception by relatives (25). The results of our investigations follow in the table below (see Table 35).

The coding of the attitudes of relatives is rather subjective, but the same principle of evaluation has been used for all outcome groups. We have tried to form our opinions partly from what the patients tell and partly from information given by relatives.

The majority of relatives we have considered to have friendly, helpful attitudes. We are well aware that unconscious hostile feelings may be present, but have only coded hostility when openly expressed. Clear-cut, overprotecting attitudes we found

TABLE 35

ATTITUDE OF RELATIVES TOWARDS PATIENTS BEFORE ADMISSION AND AT RE-EXAMINATION

Attitude of Relatives Towards Patients Before Admission and at Re-examination	Chronic Schizophrenics in Gaustad Hospital		Chronic Schizophrenics Outside Hospitals		Improved Schizophrenics		Recovered Schizophrenics		Manic-depressive Psychoses		Reactive Psychoses		Total	
	Before adm.	At re-ex.	Before adm.	At re-ex.	Before adm.	At re-ex.	Before adm.	At re-ex.	Before adm.	At re-ex.	Before adm.	At re-ex.	Before adm.	At re-ex.
Friendly, helping	63	25	67	65	66	59	74	81	85	82	70	75	70	62
Overprotective	1	0	0	3	1	1	4	1	0	0	2	1	2	1
Indifferent	10	31	17	17	12	16	8	10	13	18	9	13	11	18
Hostile	12	10	9	4	9	10	10	4	2	0	17	4	11	6
No relations	14	34	7	11	12	14	4	4	0	0	2	7	6	13
Total	100	100	100	100	100	100	100	100	100	100	100	100	100	100
No. of cases	118	118	75	75	86	86	96	96	61	61	119	119	555	555

only rarely. But the distinction between "friendly," "helpful" and "overprotecting" is rather difficult. The present sample consists mostly of acute psychoses. In delayed admissions *Ödegård* has shown that a late admission is often related to overprotective attitudes (136).

Before admission the relatives of manic-depressive psychoses in particular showed friendly and helpful attitudes (85 per cent). Then followed the recovered schizophrenics with 74 per cent and the smallest percentage (63 per cent) was found for the chronic schizophrenics in Gaustad Hospital. Overprotective and indifferent attitudes showed no particular relationship to clinical outcome. In the total material 11 per cent had hostile attitudes. The percentage varied from 2 per cent in the manic-depressive to 17 per cent in the reactive psychoses, where this factor was significantly more frequent than in the other outcome groups (P < 0.02). Among forty patients with no relations with relatives thirty-three developed schizophrenic defects, and the chronic schizophrenics in Gaustad Hospital had significantly more such cases than the other outcome groups (P < 0.001).

At re-examination friendly and helpful attitudes were considerably less frequent in those with schizophrenic defects than in the other outcome groups (P < 0.001). Still the manic-depressives have most relatives with positive attitudes. Then followed the recovered schizophrenics and the reactive psychoses. The chronic schizophrenics in Gaustad Hospital had few friendly and helping relatives. One must, however, take into consideration that many have been given a trial at home, and that aggressive behavior is frequent in this group. Our data may indicate that the chronic schizophrenics in Gaustad Hospital, to a great extent, are "forgotten" by their relatives, who mostly have indifferent attitudes to the patients, or they have no relations at all.

Hostile attitudes appear to be less frequent at re-examination than before admission. The difference is marked in the reactive group, where the psychotic reaction was often precipitated by conflicts with close relatives.

Many of the improved schizophrenics have no connection with relatives. This corresponds to their tendency to live alone, predominantly in lodgings and hostels. Also clinically the improved schizophrenics often give the impression of wanting to avoid contact with other people.

The attitudes of relatives towards patients is illustrated with a few case histories. An example of an overprotective attitude is No. 16001, female, born 1924. Her mother was very dominant and the patient had no opportunity to develop her own initiative. As the mother considered her child too sensitive for ordinary public school, the patient went to an anthroposophic private school. During the war the family moved from the center to the outskirts of Oslo. This somewhat increased the distance to school, and for this reason the mother took the patient out of school and taught her herself. In 1945 the patient was admitted to Gaustad Hospital. Outstanding in the clinical picture were philosophical speculations and delusions about being God. Her mother was quite troublesome at the hospital, interfering with every detail in the management of the patient, and wanting to prescribe the treatment which the patient ought to receive. The patient was discharged as insane with the diagnosis of schizophrenia. She left, against the advice of the hospital, because her mother did not consider Gaustad Hospital the right place for such a sensitive person as her daughter.

In 1956 the patient was re-examined in her home. She now felt that the main reason why she had become ill was that she was too childish and dependent, and had been so much at home that she was unable to associate with other young people. The megalomanic religious delusions she interpreted as an over-compensation of feelings of inferiority and lack of self-confidence. Soon after discharge the patient went abroad and educated herself as a designer of textiles. She had now returned to Oslo, where she had a flat which she shared with two girl friends. Now she felt that she had learned to be independent and that she had become more mature. There was a Bohemian appearance about the patient in dress as well as in manners. In the case history she was described as having a schizoid premorbid personality, but such personality traits could not be found at all on re-examination. The patient was clinically classified as a recovered schizophrenic.

A typical example of hostile attitudes on the part of relatives is No. 15220. Male, born 1904. He was married, but the marriage was full of conflicts. His wife had sexual intercourse with other men, and left him several times. The patient was treated in Gaustad Hospital during the war. When he returned home his wife was living with a German soldier in the flat and the patient was thrown out. He subsequently divorced her. He was re-examined in 1957. In the following years he consulted the examiner several times for neurasthenic and psychosomatic complaints (lumbago and pain in the genital organs). The diagnosis was one of a reactive psychosis.

No. 16890. Female, born 1897. Her husband, of a brutal nature and addicted to drink, had been sentenced for burglaries. In 1948 he chased her out of the house, and shortly afterwards she was admitted to Gaustad Hospital. When re-examined in 1957 she had divorced and lived with a sister. The patient was strongly neurotic, had a considerably reduced working ability and the diagnosis of reactive psychosis could be catamnestically verified.

Examples of patients without family connections have already been mentioned. We would refer to the cases No. 14967 (page 90), No. 16296 (page 94), No. 14837 (page 95), No. 14736 (page 111), and No. 17116 (page 112). In chapter II we have presented case histories of patients belonging to various clinical subgroups. Most of these had no contact with relatives. Severe deterioration has been the main reason why they have been "forgotten" by their relatives. The degree to which relatives preserve friendly and helping attitudes, in spite of all difficulties, may be more surprising. This is illustrated by a few examples.

No. 16497. Female, born 1914, was one of the few cases with severe schizophrenic deterioration seen at home. She was treated in the hospital in 1947 and re-examined in 1959. The patient had, for a short period, been placed in family care as insane. But her sister thought that the patient suffered at the farm and took her to live with her. The patient spoke quite incoherently and could not give a single adequate answer to questions. She related that her heart was torn out, her back broken and her eyes running down her face. The patient needed care and supervision in every way and was a great burden on her sister, who was at work during the day, but apart from some indecent speech the patient was good-humored and amenable. Ataraxic drugs were prescribed in order to make an attempt to ameliorate the condition of the patient. Her sister preferred to care for her as long as she could manage it.

No. 16753. Female, born 1907, was treated in Gaustad Hospital in 1948. When re-examined in 1959 she presented a severe schizophrenic deterioration. She sat in a chair, spoke incoherently and could give no answers to questions. She moved her body stereotypically, and she had scratched herself in the face and under the arms. Apart from the stereotype movements she had a marked catatonic stiffness. Her parents had to help her in every way, and because of the patient's incoherent speech and completely disordered behavior they were reluctant to let others see her outside the house. Only in the summer would the patient sit for a short while in their garden.

No. 16248. Male, born 1908, was admitted to Gaustad Hospital in 1946. In 1959 he lived with his sister and mother, and had not done a day's work for the last thirteen years. He used to lie in bed most of the day, and became angry if his relatives asked him to work. When the patient was confronted with this, he merely remarked that his family did quite well without his working and that he was too ill to work.

No. 17150. Male, born 1916, was admitted to Gaustad Hospital in 1949. When re-examined in 1956, he was unstable in work and could not meet his economic responsibilities. His family supported him in every way and his sisters had spent most of their savings upon him.

No. 14868. Female, born 1914, was admitted to Gaustad Hospital in 1939 for paranoid schizophrenia. In 1959 she was re-examined in her home. Since discharge she had been supported by her parents, who now were over seventy years old. The patient had been very difficult, and often dissatisfied and angry with her parents. Her parents wanted her to submit to medical treatment, but the patient was very angry with the doctors, and they would not readmit her to the hospital against her will.

12. ATTITUDE OF PATIENTS TOWARDS HOSPITALIZATION

The attitude of patients towards hospitalization, doctors and nursing staff is obviously important for after-care problems. The results of our investigations are presented in Table 36 (see table).

TABLE 36

ATTITUDE OF PATIENTS TOWARDS HOSPITALIZATION

Attitude of Patients Towards Hospitalization	Chronic Schizophrenics in Gaustad Hospital	Chronic Schizophrenics Outside Hospitals	Improved Schizophrenics	Recovered Schizophrenics	Manic-depressive Psychoses	Reactive Psychoses	Total
Appreciative	6	10	24	67	47	81	235
Indifferent	96	41	47	24	8	18	234
Complaining	16	24	15	5	6	20	86
Total	118	75	86	96	61	119	555

On the basis of the interviews at re-examination we have tried to evaluate how the patients look upon their hospital stay. As "appreciative" we have coded those who were thankful for treatment and what the doctors and nursing staff had done for them. In the complaining group we have included those who strongly criticized their hospitalization, treatment, doctors or nursing personnel. The remaining we have coded as indifferent, even if they may afterwards have had feelings of inferiority or social discrimination. The latter aspects will be dealt with in the next section.

Appreciative attitudes are found considerably less often in those with schizophrenic defects than in the other groups (P < 0.001). The greatest percentage of appreciative attitudes was found in the manic-depressive psychoses (77 per cent). The few who complained about their hospitalization had manic periods and no complete insight afterwards. Their complaints were mainly that hospitalization should not have been necessary. Also most of the recovered schizophrenics were thankful for the treatment they received in the hospital (70 per cent). Only five of them complained, and mainly because they considered treatment in mental hospital unnecessary. Along similar lines several in the reactive group also complained. Predominantly their negative attitudes towards hospitalization resulted from psychopathic outward projection. Nevertheless, 68 per cent were appreciative.

Many of the improved and chronic schizophrenics complained about their hospital stay. In these cases the attitudes tended to be related either to psychotic ideas or to lack of insight into such ideas. Most of the improved and chronic schizophrenics were rather indifferent about their hospital stay. We feel that this indifference mainly results from lack of insight or emotional blunting. Especially the chronic schizophrenics in Gaustad Hospital were mostly so affectively flattened that they expressed no particular opinion about their hospital stay. The chronic schizophrenics with hostile attitudes towards the hospital are emotionally the least deteriorated, and have consequently better chances than the indifferent to live outside mental hospitals.

When we visited the patients in their homes, a kind reception and appreciative attitudes towards the hospital strongly indicated a favorable outcome of the psychosis. It was often rather difficult to obtain re-examination of the complaining patients and also of several of the indifferent. A great deal of those with poor outcome of the illness could not be expected to answer to written questionnaires. This expectation was also confirmed in respect to answers of letters from patients outside the geographical area chosen for personal re-examination (Chapter I). Our analysis of the attitudes of patients strongly supports the assumption that personal follow-up is essential for obtaining a true picture of prognosis in follow-up studies. It seems also that those who are most in need of after-care, have as a rule indifferent or complaining attitudes towards hospitalization.

We will illustrate the attitudes of patients towards hospitalization with a few case histories.

No. 17161. Female, born 1914, was treated in Gaustad Hospital in 1949. When re-examined in her home in 1959 the patient presented a slight schizophrenic deterioration. She was extremely suspicious and delivered long, nearly incoherent complaints about hospitals, doctors, police, and, in particular, Gaustad Hospital. She would not be spied upon and inconvenienced by doctors and police as long as she paid her taxes and her rent. After calming down, she related that she had night work and associated with nobody in her leisure time. Spontaneously she remarked: "Friends are the worst of evils. One never knows where one is with them."

No. 15553. Male, born 1916, was treated in the hospital in 1943 for paranoid schizophrenia and discharged as insane. During a visit to the home in 1956 his seventy-three year old father was encountered. He became very anxious about the visit and said that if the patient should learn that a doctor from Gaustad Hospital had been let into the house he would be furious and give his father no peace. The patient was very embittered about the hospital stay. If he saw doctors or ambulances he made long detours. He thought that he had been destroyed by the shock treatments. Before admission he worked as an engineer, and now he had simple unskilled work. We had to promise the father to make no attempts at personal re-examination (this patient, therefore, is not included in the statistical analysis of attitudes).

No. 16437. Female, born 1911. The patient was treated in the hospital in 1947. When re-examined in 1956, she was classified as an improved schizophrenic and was self-supporting. The patient was very angry about her hospital stay, and thought she was treated like an animal and not like a human being. She remarked that the Medical Superintendent thought more of his post than his patients. Her nervous illness, she claimed, should have been treated with psychotherapy, which she had received prior to admission (without effect).

Most of the hospitalized schizophrenic cases reported in chapter II were rather indifferent about their hospitalization. The main reason for this was severe deterioration.

No. 14951. Male, born 1898, was treated in the hospital in 1940. He suffered from a short-lasting schizophrenic psychosis, precipitated by war events. On a visit to his home in 1956 his wife was encountered. She related that the patient considered his admission to the mental hospital for such a short mental breakdown as completely unnecessary. In the small town where they lived people had talked about his having been insane. This was so embarrassing that they moved to another town. Now the patient was well-adapted in all aspects. We had to promise his wife not

to see him personally and stir up the memories of the unhappy
episode, which now lay sixteen years back in time (this patient is,
therefore, not included in the statistical analysis of attitudes).

No. 14954. Male, born 1907, was also treated in Gaustad
Hospital for a psychosis with schizophrenic symptoms, which broke
out in connection with war events in 1940. When re-examined in
1956 he stated that the hospital admission was unnecessary and
that he was brutally treated.

No. 16957. Male, born 1911, was treated in Gaustad Hospital
in 1949 for a psychosis with schizophrenic symptoms, which was
precipitated by sexual conflicts. He wanted to marry a domestic
servant on their farm, but his parents objected, as they did not
consider the woman as fit for a farmer's wife. In 1952 he fell in
love with another domestic servant on the farm. As he feared the
opinions of his parents he became depressed and sought voluntary
admission to the hospital. He was re-examined in his home in
1956. After discharge he married the last-mentioned woman,
had two children, and their marriage was very happy. The patient
was appreciative of the treatment, received the examiner in a
friendly manner, and took great pride in showing his well kept
farm. In particular he was proud of his pigs, which had received
several prizes. The patient could be classified as recovered schizophrenic, but had several relatives with schizophrenic deterioration.

In connection with quarreling with the neighbors he became
depressed with hypochondriacal sensations in 1959. After having
been depressed for three months he came to the hospital in order
to seek advice. This time he recovered after ambulatory treatment
with ataraxic drugs (truxal and chlorpromazine). He was very
thankful, especially for having a return of his love for fine pigs.
This patient illustrates the rule about the association of appreciative attitudes and favorable outcome and also the advantages of
contact with the hospital.

13. FEELINGS ABOUT HAVING BEEN
A MENTAL HOSPITAL PATIENT

In clinical practice it is well known that patients often have
feelings of inferiority or social discrimination because of having
been mental hospital patients. Such feelings pose important prob-

lems for after-care programs. We also assumed that these feelings might be differently related to clinical outcome types. The results of our investigations are given in the table below (see Table 37).

TABLE 37

FEELINGS ABOUT HAVING BEEN A MENTAL HOSPITAL PATIENT

Feelings About Having Been a Mental Hospital Patient	Chronic Schizophrenics in Gaustad Hospital	Chronic Schizophrenics Outside Hospitals	Improved Schizophrenics	Recovered Schizophrenics	Manic-depressive Psychoses	Reactive Psychoses	Total
Feelings of inferiority or social discrimination	3	21	29	23	10	36	122
Essentially no uneasiness	115	54	57	73	51	83	433
Total	118	75	86	96	61	119	555

We have systematically tried to ask the patients about their feelings of having been a mental hospital patient. Feelings of inferiority or social discrimination we have only coded when clearly expressed by patients.

It is striking that the chronic schizophrenics in Gaustad Hospital with a few exceptions expressed no uneasiness. The reason for this is predominantly emotional blunting and autistic absorption in the psychotic world. Even if complaining about hospitalization and asking to be discharged, they do not express feelings of inferiority or stigma because they are mental hospital patients.

The chronic schizophrenics outside mental hospitals, to a great extent, consider their difficulties of adaptation result from having been in a mental hospital. The same is the case with the improved schizophrenics. These patients have not sufficient insight to understand what is wrong with themselves. Apparently the most acceptable formulation for them is that they are like others, but have difficulties because they were so unfortunate as to be admitted to a mental hospital.

Most of the manic-depressives felt essentially no uneasiness about their hospitalization. Predominantly they tended to regard their psychotic periods as something like ordinary somatic diseases.

Several of the recovered schizophrenics and those with reactive psychoses revealed strong feelings of inferiority because they had been admitted to the hospital. In the reactive group some psychopaths also related their problems to social discrimination.

Our general conclusion is that the feelings about having been a mental hospital patient are very differently related to prognosis for various clinical outcome groups. For after-care programmes it would be important to modify the feelings of inferiority and social discrimination.

With exception of No. 14762 (page 16) the nineteen deteriorated schizophrenics reported in chapter II expressed no uneasiness about having been mental hospital patients. These case histories may serve as typical examples of schizophrenics re-examined in the hospital, who mostly are too ill to express any feelings of stigma.

No. 14837 (page 95) and No. 17116 (page 112) may illustrate how schizophrenics outside mental hospitals tend to feel social discrimination. Another example is No. 15362, female, born 1908. The patient was treated in the hospital in 1942 and re-examined in 1956. Prior to admission she kept company with German occupation soldiers and had an illegitimate child by one of them. She lived in a dirty and badly furnished room and became very angry when she heard that the examiner from Gaustad Hospital had come. She felt that there had been no reason for the hospitalization. She claimed she was tortured in the hospital and that nurses and doctors laughed at her and said they could kill people and awaken them to life again. Since discharge she had been working and supporting herself as well as her son, but she complained that people talked about her on the job and circulated evil rumors concerning her. Her son, she said, was accused of all kinds of knavish tricks and even thefts. She felt that she and her son were being persecuted because she had been in Gaustad Hospital.

We will also give some examples of patients with a non-schizophrenic course of illness. No. 16380. Female, born 1903, was treated in the hospital in 1946. When re-examined in 1957 a diagnosis of querulent paranoia could be catamnestically established. She made a long speech about all the "injustice" she had experienced, and thought the hospital admission was due to a plot of her enemies. The patient felt it especially humilitating that she had been discharged as "insane," and that it had placed a stigma upon her. Since discharge she had quarrelled with the health authorities about having the medical certificate set aside. During the war she had been a member of the Quisling party and there was a huge pile of documents about her fight for revindication. The patient considered the follow-up an insult, and afterwards wrote a complaining letter to the hospital.

No. 14822. Male, born 1906, had been admitted to the hospital in 1939 for a reactive psychosis and was re-examined in 1959. Since discharge he had suffered from feelings of inferiority and at times from tendencies to ideas of reference. Often he had contacted the hospital for advice, and he received the examiner in a friendly fashion. Yet afterwards he sent a letter and complained that the follow-up had opened his old wounds. This was especially hard on him because he had recently suffered a great personal defeat in competition with a younger and less qualified man about a better job.

The previously mentioned cases No. 16910 (page 95), No. 15101 (page 97), and No. 14951 (page 120) may also serve as examples of patients feeling themselves inferior because of having been in mental hospitals.

During our follow-up we took great pains to avoid stirring up the sore feelings of patients about their disease. For patients who were readmitted after the follow-up, we always tried to evaluate if the relapses might be set in relation to the interviews.

No. 14929. Male, born 1916, was treated in the hospital in 1940. When re-examined in September 1956, he was classified as a recovered schizophrenic. He enjoyed a happy marriage with four children and had made good occupational progress. Because of his illness he had strong feelings of inferiority, which increased after the follow-up interview. In March 1957, a minor accident occurred in the railroad district where he worked as a foreman. He could not possibly be blamed for the accident, but started to think that as a former mental hospital patient he was incapable of having such responsible work involving control of the security of the railroad line. The patient also falsely interpreted remarks from the examiner in this direction. In May 1957, he became psychotic and was readmitted. After a short stay in the hospital he could be discharged as recovered.

No. 16823. Male, born 1921, was treated in the hospital in 1948 for periodic catatonia. When re-examined in 1956 he presented a general psychic lameness characteristic of such mild defects. He had married and feared very much that his parents-in-law would get to know about his mental illness. He had experienced many inconveniences after his hospital stay. On the job he felt that the others paid no attention to his opinions and considered him as an inferior person. In 1957 he was re-admitted for a new catatonic episode. His brother could tell that the patient had reacted strongly to the follow-up interview, which revived what he had tried to forget. This brother had also been treated in Gaustad Hospital for periodic catatonia, presented a mild defect, had married without telling his wife about the mental illness and was considerably distressed himself by the follow-up interview. Furthermore, there were four schizophrenic uncles and aunts and one schizophrenic half-brother in the family.

No. 16573. Female, born 1921, was treated in Gaustad Hospital in 1947 for periodic catatonia. When re-examined in 1956 she had minor schizophrenic personality changes. She had made good advances in her job and had recently acquired a new apartment for herself, but she was not happy with her living conditions, lacked contacts with friends and thought her life was rather empty. She considered her mental illness as a stigma, and wept when talking about it. In 1957 the patient was re-admitted to the hospital for a catatonic relapse. Her father could tell that she had brooded much after the follow-up interview, and felt that this might have played a role in the precipitation of the relapse. Other possible causes were perhaps more likely, however. In 1947 the psychotic period came in relation to a love affair, and now she had again had an unhappy love experience. A brother had also suffered from several periods of periodic catatonia.

No. 15175. Female, born 1892, was treated in Gaustad Hospital in 1945 for manic-depressive psychosis and re-examined in 1959. In 1957 she had been treated in another psychiatric hospital for depression. Apart from periodic sleep disturbances she was quite well and received the examiner amiably. Her relatives could tell that the patient brooded about why she was interviewed and the following day appeared depressed. As the depression gradually increased the patient was admitted to a psychiatric clinic four weeks after the follow-up interview. Although the time interval between the follow-up interview and the psychotic relapse was short, we are inclined to assume that there was no causal relation. The patient had several minor nervous periods, which used to break out rather acutely without relation to any external precipitating events.

14. COMPLICATIONS OF MENTAL DISEASE

It is obvious that severe complications of mental disease such as attempts at suicide, aggressive behavior or criminality will increase the chance of commitment to a mental hospital. For delayed admission *Ödegård* found it remarkable that acts of violence or other serious offences were not registered in the total material (136). Complications before as well as after admission should be expected to be important for the chances of discharge and post-hospital adjustment. *Harris et al* reported that 59 per cent of schizophrenics dangerous to themselves or others were found in the long-stay hospital group. Among those with no socially embarrassing symptoms at all only 4 per cent were found to have spent two or more years in the hospital during the follow-up period (62). Our results are presented in the following table (see Table 38).

As seen from the table, we have coded more factors than patients. The reason for this is that some cases have more than one type of complication.

Before admission attempts at suicide were more frequent in

TABLE 38

COMPLICATIONS OF MENTAL DISEASE BEFORE ADMISSION AND AT RE-EXAMINATION

Complications of Mental Disease Before Admission and at Re-examination (After Admission.)	Chronic Schizophrenics in Gaustad Hospital		Chronic Schizophrenics Outside Hospitals		Improved Schizophrenics		Recovered Schizophrenics		Manic-depressive Psychoses		Reactive Psychoses		Total	
	Before adm.	At re-ex.	Before adm.	At re-ex.	Before adm.	At re-ex.	Before adm.	At re-ex.	Before adm.	At re-ex.	Before adm.	At re-ex.	Before adm.	At re-ex.
Attemps at suicide	11	10	9	3	7	6	8	1	26	5	26	4	15	5
Aggressive behaviour	44	68	22	9	16	3	14	3	10	1	18	4	22	19
Criminality	8	5	8	1	10	1	3	2	0	5	5	4	6	3
No serious complications	37	17	61	87	67	90	75	94	64	89	51	88	57	73
Total	100	100	100	100	100	100	100	100	100	100	100	100	100	100
No. of cases (complications)	125	131	77	75	86	87	96	96	61	61	124	121	569	571

the affective psychoses than in the schizophrenic groups (P <
0.001). In the manic-depressive psychoses 26 per cent and in the
reactive psychoses 26 per cent had made attempts at suicide.
Taking into consideration that the reactive psychoses had most
suicides (Chapter III), their attempts must not be taken less
seriously than those of the manic-depressives.

Only few of the manic-depressives showed aggressive behavior previous to admission. Most such behavior was found
among the chronic schizophrenics in Gaustad Hospital. In this
respect they were clearly different from the chronic schizophrenics outside mental hospitals (statistically significant at the
0.001 level). The aggressive behavior seems, however, to a great
extent to result from severe deterioration.

The chronic and improved schizophrenics had most of the
criminality before admission. The greatest percentages without
serious complications were found in the recovered schizophrenics
(75 per cent). Then followed the improved schizophrenics (67
per cent), the manic-depressive psychoses (64 per cent), the
chronic schizophrenics outside mental hospitals (61 per cent),
the reactive psychoses (51 per cent), and the chronic schizophrenics in Gaustad Hospital (37 per cent).

After admission all kinds of complications were most frequent among the chronic schizophrenics in Gaustad Hospital.
Only twenty-three of them had no serious complications. It was
rather unexpected that as many as thirteen of them had made
attempts at suicide. According to Chapter III there were only
five suicides in the total material of schizophrenics. On the other
hand, the few attempts at suicide among patients with affective
psychoses stand somewhat in contrast to the eleven suicides in
the total material during the follow-up period. Possibly some of
our personally re-examined cases would not tell about attempts
at suicide during our interviews.

When the chronic schizophrenics outside mental hospitals
are compared with those in Gaustad Hospital, the differences with
respect to aggressive behavior are even greater than before admission (P < 0.01). Criminal behavior played a smaller role after
than before admission, and this was due to less criminality in
those with schizophrenic defects.

We can conclude that aggressive behavior has probably been the most important reason why chronic schizophrenics stay in the hospital.

Although aggressive behavior was very common, in no case did this lead to manslaughter or serious bodily injury. The most severe complication was in No. 14729. Male, born 1915. He was treated in Gaustad Hospital in 1938 and re-examined in 1959. The patient was a psychopath who had received psychoanalytic treatment for his personal maladjustment. After an attempt to murder his psychoanalyst, he was imprisoned. In prison he developed a reactive psychosis and was transferred to Gaustad Hospital. Because of aggressive behavior he was later, for several years, in another mental hospital. At re-examination his social adaptation was rather marginal. He was very polite, eager to please the examiner and by no means gave an aggressive impression. The patient had married and seemed to be completely dominated by his wife, who was rather suspicious of the examiner's intentions.

Among the criminal cases there were some who had committed serious crimes in German service during the war. No. 16316. Male, born 1923, had taken part in execution of Norwegian patriots and the prosecution demanded the death penalty. When the patient heard this, he reacted with a hysterical confused stupor and was admitted to Gaustad Hospital. He was sentenced to imprisonment for life, but was released in 1950. When re-examined in 1957 he was socially well-adapted, had a good job, a wife and children, regretted what he had done, and had completely broken with the past.

No. 16192. Male, born 1907, had worked for Gestapo during the war. He took part in the executions and tortured the prisoners with whip, thumbscrews and red-hot irons. After the prosecution had demanded the death sentence, the patient became psychotic and was admitted to Gaustad Hospital in 1946. He was released from prison in 1953 and re-examined in 1959. The hospital diagnosis was one of reactive psychosis, but in 1959 the patient presented typical schizophrenic personality changes. Speech was distorted and the facial expression stiff with grimaces. During the psychosis he considered himself to be a great inventor and the

Biblical Melchisedek. The patient commented that in a difficult situation it may be convenient to hide oneself behind the mask of another person.

The criminality of the schizophrenics previous to admission had mainly been minor offences, such as thefts, which often were combined with begging and vagrancy. A typical example is No. 15211. Male, born 1909. In 1942 he became psychotic while imprisoned for thefts and burglary and was admitted to Gaustad Hospital. After discharge he had lived a vagabond life and it was extremely difficult to get information about his address. His sister informed us that during the winter the patient used to be in Oslo. He was known to be a beggar and slept in the open air, in bomb shelters or in empty railroad wagons. In his appearance he used to be so dirty and eccentric that people were afraid of him. During summer he generally did farm work. At last we found him on a farm, where he was placed in public care. The patient related in 1956 that since discharge he had been arrested several times for thefts and drunkenness. Prison life he considered fairly good. His only objection was the closed doors. He led a lonely life, would have nothing to do with his family and felt quite correctly that they too would have nothing to do with him.

No. 14823. Male, born 1905, was a vagrant who had several times been sentenced for thefts. He was admitted to the hospital in 1939. Since that time he had been practically continually in the hospital and had no opportunity to steal.

No. 14879. Male, born 1898, had often committed petty thefts, and had been placed in a labor camp because of begging and vagrancy. Here he became psychotic and was admitted to Gaustad Hospital in 1939. After discharge he continued his asocial existence until he was readmitted in 1949. Since that time he was continually in the hospital.

No. 17088. Male, born 1928, in the middle of the day broke into the house of a neighbor and stole a cigar. The whole act was completely without motive and led to the recognition of his schizophrenic illness.

No. 15638. Male, born 1922, had prior to admission made

an attempt at rape. After his first admission in 1943 he was mostly in Gaustad Hospital. He was released to family care, but had to be readmitted because of aggressive behavior towards women.

No. 16652. Male, born 1919, prior to admisison was sentenced for violence and drunkenness. His family tried several times to have him at home. But each time he had to be readmitted for aggressive behavior.

An example of the danger of underestimating the risks of suicide in patients with reactive psychoses is No. 16681. Female, born 1913. The premorbid personality was hysterical with a tendency to dramatize. Since puberty she had suffered from psychosomatic complaints, such as headache, constipation and dysmenorrhea. She had for years been anxious, often felt tired, stayed in bed for long periods, and had not felt strong enough to take any jobs away from home. In 1938 she made an attempt at suicide and during the following years often told her relatives that she would take her own life. She was admitted to Gaustad Hospital in the beginning of 1948 after having related that she had swallowed a solution of nicotine sulphate. The relatives, as well as her doctor, suspected the patient of lying and merely wanting to make a dramatic episode. In the hospital the patient was depressed, but gave no impression of being really suicidal. She also had two short periods of confusional excitements which appeared typically hysterical. She told of strong conflicts with her mother, who always had been very dominating. Since the age of sixteen the patient had sexual relations with a man who wanted to marry her. But she considered herself too nervous to venture into marriage and saw no solution of this basic conflict. After convulsive treatment the patient was discharged as improved at the end of 1948 with the diagnosis of hysteric reactive psychosis. At home she soon fell back into her habitual neurotic state and tendency to depression. In 1951 she was readmitted and after three months discharged as improved. This time she had made no attempt at suicide, but said all her life she had had suicidal thoughts.

During the follow-up we received the information that the patient had committed suicide by strangulation in 1953. Her relatives told us that in the last months previous to the suicide the patient was more than usually depressed and often spoke about taking her own life. But she had for so many years spoken about this that her relatives were not alarmed. Our impression is that this patient was so habitually occupied with suicidal thoughts that it was extremely difficult to protect her against herself by means of admission to the hospital.

15. PHYSICAL HEALTH

From our study of acute affective psychoses it appeared that the manic-depressives had considerably less psychosomatic diseases than the reactive psychoses (8).

Among "psychosomatic diseases" we have included gastric and duodenal ulcers, unspecific dyspepsia, bronchial asthma, Graves' disease, diabetes, cardiac neuroses, sciatica and lumbago, cephalalgia, eczema, hypertension, and severe dysmenorrhea. We will present our findings for the personally seen patients in the table below (see Table 39).

We made no attempt to analyze the occurrence of all kinds of somatic disease, but limited ourselves to psychosomatic disease and chronic disabling somatic disease. When the conditions mentioned were not found, we have coded good bodily health, even if they had severe intercurrent somatic diseases.

It is seen from Table 39 that psychosomatic disease before admission was predominantly found in the reactive group. They had also more disabling somatic disease than the other outcome groups. The reactive psychoses had significantly more persons with psychosomatic disease than the other outcome groups ($P <$ 0.001), and, as expected, also more than the manic-depressives ($P < 0.01$).

At re-examination the number of patients with psychosomatic disease and chronic disabling somatic disease has increased. Now the differences between reactive psychoses and manic-depressive psychoses with respect to psychosomatic disease are statistically significant at the 0.001 level, but the manic-depressives have the greatest percentage of chronic disabling somatic disease (11 per cent).

Several case histories cited in other connections may serve as examples of the tendency of patients with reactive psychoses to develop psychosomatic diseases. Such are No. 16400 (page 40),

TABLE 39

PHYSICAL HEALTH BEFORE ADMISSION AND AT RE-EXAMINATION

Bodily Health Before Admission and at Re-examination (After Admission)	Chronic Schizophrenics in Gaustad Hospital		Chronic Schizophrenics Outside Hospitals		Improved Schizophrenics		Recovered Schizophrenics		Manic-depressive Psychoses		Reactive Psychoses		Total	
	Before adm.	At re-ex.	Before adm.	At re-ex.	Before adm.	At re-ex.	Before adm.	At re-ex.	Before adm.	At re-ex.	Before adm.	At re-ex.	Before adm.	At re-ex.
Good bodily health	97	92	91	88	91	86	91	80	87	79	63	56	86	79
Psychosomatic disease	3	8	8	8	7	10	4	14	10	10	30	36	11	16
Chronic disabling somatic disease	0	0	1	4	2	4	5	6	3	11	7	8	3	5
Total	100	100	100	100	100	100	100	100	100	100	100	100	100	100
No. of cases	118	118	75	75	86	86	96	96	61	61	119	119	555	555

No. 14940 (page 40), No. 16392 (page 45), No. 16774 (page 98), and No. 15220 (page 115).

16. OUTLOOK ON LIFE

From the interviews at re-examination we have tried to evaluate if the patients have satisfactory or lowered enjoyment of life. This factor has especially been stressed by *Ström-Olsen* as important in a multidimensional analysis of the outcome of illness (167). We place our findings in the following table (see Table 40).

TABLE 40

OUTLOOK ON LIFE AT RE-EXAMINATION

Enjoyment of Life at Re-examination	Chronic Schizophrenics in Gaustad Hospital	Chronic Schizophrenics Outside Hospitals	Improved Schizophrenics	Recovered Schizophrenics	Manic-depressive Psychoses	Reactive Psychoses	Total
Satisfactory	54	23	33	78	50	60	298
Lowered	64	52	53	18	11	59	257
Total	118	75	86	96	61	119	555

Compared with the other outcome groups, the manic-depressives reveal a greater tendency to express satisfactory enjoyment of life (P < 0.001). The recovered schizophrenics, for the most part, also have statisfactory enjoyment of life. Those with reactive psychoses were considerably more dissatisfied with their conditions of life than the manic-depressives (P < 0.001). The improved schizophrenics and the chronic schizophrenics outside mental hospitals suffer more from their disorders than the chronic schizophrenics in Gaustad Hospital, but the differences were only statistically significant at the 0.05 level. The clinical analysis shows that many chronic schizophrenics in Gaustad Hospital feel well because they are emotionally blunted and euphoric. For this reason it is easily understandable that lowered enjoyment of life in chronic schizophrenics is a favorable aspect with respect to succeeding in living outside a mental hospital.

We will present a few case histories in order to illustrate what the patients themselves think about their conditions in life.

An example of decreased enjoyment of life among chronic schizophrenics living outside mental hospitals is No. 15527, born 1906, was admitted to the hospital in 1943. She was married and had two children. As the patient was very jealous of her husband, she would not go home to her family on discharge, but took jobs as a domestic servant far away from her home. When re-examined in 1959, she related that she had suffered severe persecution from her husband and his family and that even her own family had done her much evil. She had all the time since discharge heard voices uttering unpleasant accusations. Her life had been an incessant struggle against tremendous suffering.

No. 16496. Male, born 1903, was admitted to Gaustad Hospital in 1947 for paranoid schizophrenia of several years' duration and discharged after six months. When re-examined in 1960, he related that he had heard voices all the time since discharge. These voices shouted unpleasantly to him. He believed his whole body was poisoned by phosphorus. He received poor relief and was unable to work, not only because of mental illness, but also as he suffered from heart disease. In the summer he slept in the woods. During winter he slept in hostels when he had money, and often on staircases. His greatest wish was to get a room for himself, and we sent a recommendation to the proper authorities. The patient said that life had been hard on him and that he suffered very much.

No. 16935. Male, born 1916, was treated in Gaustad Hospital in 1949 for paranoid schizophrenia. When re-examined in 1959 he related that people "spoke badly" about him, accused him of crimes and wanted to injure him. The reason he gave for this was that he had been treated in Gaustad Hospital. The patient received poor relief, but most of the money had to be used to pay for his room in a hostel. As to food, he could barely afford bread and soup and there was nothing left for clothes. The patient was put in touch with a social welfare organization which helped him with clothes and food tickets for dinner.

No. 16368. Female, born 1895, was admitted to the hospital in 1946 and discharged in 1947 as recovered. When re-examined in her home in 1959, she was classified as suffering from paranoid schizophrenia. She thought that people everywhere could hear what she and her husband discussed. People "spoke badly" about her in the streets, so that she did not venture to go out. The patient suffered very much from her hallucinations and sensitive delusions of reference. Her husband had a pension and had to give up an extra job in order to care for his wife. She protested very much against being readmitted and ataraxic drugs were prescribed in order to reduce her sufferings.

No. 15955. Male, born 1916, was admitted to Gaustad Hospital in 1945 for paranoid schizophrenia, was discharged as insane to his home after two months, and re-examined in 1959. He related that he often heard voices which he considered as divine guidance. He was active in religious life and felt that this gave his life a purpose. The patient was a clever worker, had saved much money, and was quite satisfied with his conditions of life. He was not interested in taking ataraxic drugs in order to reduce the effect of the hallucinations. On the contrary we had the impression that he had converted the hallucinatory experiences into a kind of inspiring support.

Another example of a schizophrenic patient who evaluated psychotic experiences positively was No. 15328. Male, born 1888. Prior to admission (1942) he had been psychotic for ten years. He was discharged in 1945 as insane. When re-examined in 1959 he considered himself to be a prophet with revelations. He predicted that the world would end in 1960. Then he would be one of the 20,000 Christian revivalists. This made him quite happy, although he barely existed on an old age pension, had no contacts with friends or relatives, and lived in a hostel where he shared room with many persons who were often drunk and obscene.

As a rule, however, chronic schizophrenics with satisfactory enjoyment of life, had considerable emotional blunting. All the severely deteriorated cases reported in Chapter II may serve as examples of this.

Patients with reactive psychoses usually have reduced enjoyment of life because of neurotic symptoms. For example, the previously presented cases No. 16400 (page 40), No. 14940 (page 40), No. 16392 (page 45), No. 16774 (page 98), No. 16950 (page 98), No. 15220 (page 115), and No. 16890 (page 116).

The rule that manic-depressives have satisfactory enjoyment of life holds true even for cases with many psychotic periods. No. 16689 has already been mentioned on page 46. No. 15188. Female born 1913, was admitted to Gaustad Hospital in 1943. When re-examined in 1957 she had been treated sixteen times in another mental hospital. The patient received the examiner in a friendly manner, was open and extroverted, supported herself and expressed that she was quite happy.

No. 15569. Female, born 1911, was treated in the hospital in 1943 and re-examined in 1957. She had suffered from six psychotic periods. In 1953 she married, and her marital life was harmonious. The patient had good insight into her mental illness which she considered as something analogous to a bodily disease.

Chapter VI

HEREDITARY FACTORS AND PROGNOSIS

1. PRINCIPLES OF ANALYSIS OF HEREDITARY LOADING

No attempt has been made to carry out a complete family investigation of our patients, but in every case information about relatives known to have been insane was collected from the case history, from interviews with patients and relatives, and from the central register of the insane.

The clinical picture presented by the relatives was ascertained from their case histories (kindly loaned to us by the hospitals where they had been treated), and could be compared with the clinical condition of the patient himself. No doubt, our knowledge of psychotic relatives is incomplete, and, as we have not gathered reliable information about the total number of relatives, we cannot give any morbidity figures. We have reason to believe that our material is a representative sample with regard to the relation of the clinical picture to outcome in hospitalized psychoses, and that a comparison between probands and relatives may, therefore, be of some interest.

Genetic research has shown that the endogenous psychoses have a rather homogeneous hereditary taint (6, 73, 74, 101, 116, 118, 146, 163, 166). From the studies of *M. Bleuler* it appears that hereditary factors are of great importance for the outcome of illness in schizophrenia (21). *Leonhard* has found that his nineteen schizophrenic subgroups were hereditary very homogeneous (101). As we have subdivided the schizophrenias according to *Leonhard*, it seemed natural to test this hypothesis.

The family study was limited to grandparents, uncles, aunts, parents and siblings. There were only a few psychotic children, and their observation periods were rather short for evaluating the course of illness. Therefore, children were not included. Nephews, nieces and cousins who were rather numerous and difficult to obtain information about, were also excluded.

A comparison with the careful proband investigation of *Dahl* and *Odegard* from Gaustad Hospital shows that we have probably lost 20 per cent of the hospitalized relatives with functional psychoses (32). In a similarly studied material, *Astrup* missed only one per cent of the hospitalized functional psychoses as compared with *Dahl* and *Odegard* (9). The most likely explanation of this discrepancy is that the case histories before and during the war were less detailed with regard to hereditary taint than the material of *Astrup,* based on patients treated in the hospital during the years from 1955 to 1958. There is no reason to assume that the lost relatives should be a biased sample with regard to clinical outcome. For fifty-six of the relatives treated in mental hospitals, we did not succeed in obtaining the case histories. The reasons for this were such as hospitalization in foreign countries (in particular, The United States), case histories destroyed by fire, or not found under the given name in the files of the hospitals.

In the present material the probands have been classified on the basis of case histories, on one personal re-examination or other information as shown in Chapter I, methods of investigation. The chronic schizophrenics in the former material of Astrup had each been seen several times during three years. Thus the present proband material is less carefully subdivided than the former material of *Astrup*. The relatives were analyzed in a similar manner, so that there is a good basis for comparisons. It should be mentioned that some of the present cases belong to the former series of *Astrup,* which were studied with conditional reflex methods (9).

The following principles were used for the clinical subdivision of relatives. Some relatives with clearly catatonic symptoms, who apparently remitted, were included in the group of periodic catatonias, which as a rule has a strong tendency to remissions (see Chapter II). The other relatives with remissions were classified as affective psychoses, even if clinically some typical schizophrenic symptoms were present during the acute stage of the psychosis. Among functional psychoses there remain, then, deteriorated and improved schizophrenics. These were classified according to *Leonhard* (101).

2. GENERAL SURVEY OF HEREDITARY FACTORS

In the following table we give a survey of the genetic loading for the total material (see Table 41).

TABLE 41

GENETIC LOADING IN TOTAL GROUPS

Proband Material	*Relatives*				
	Peculiar Behaviour. Not under Psychiatric Care	*Unhospitalized. Under Care in Family Care or Nursing Homes*	*Hospitalized. Case Histories Not Available*	*Hospitalized. Case Histories Available For Functional Psychoses*	*Total of Probably Psychotic Relatives*
Deteriorated schizophrenics	163	10	18	177	368
Improved schizophrenics	56	2	4	70	132
Recovered schizophrenics	46	2	17	64	129
Reactive psychoses	46	4	9	74	133
Manic-depressive psychoses	64	0	8	48	120
Total	375	18	56	433	882

From the table it is seen that for many probably insane relatives case histories have not been available. For the vast majority of the insufficiently known relatives, there has been no hospitalization, merely information about peculiar behavior which might have been due to functional psychoses. With a similar genetic loading as in the series of *Dahl* and *Ödegård*, there should have been 615 hospitalized and 400 unhospitalized functional psychoses, whereas we have 489 hospitalized and 393 unhospitalized cases (32).

Our next step was to see for which types of relatives, sufficiently and insufficiently known genetic loading was distributed. This is demonstrated in Table 42 (see table).

TABLE 42

GENETIC LOADING IN RELATIVE GROUPS

	Genetic Loading in Relatives			
Relative Groups	*Probably Psychotic. Case Histories Not Available*	*Available Histories of Affective Psychoses*	*Available Histories of Schizophrenic Psychoses*	*Total Psychoses in Relatives*
Grandparents	57	13	5	75
Parents	103	36	36	175
Uncles and aunts	169	37	73	279
Siblings	120	80	153	353
Total	449	166	267	882

Compared with the series of *Dahl* and *Ödegård*, we have, in relation to the size of the proband materials, 93 per cent of siblings, 71 per cent of uncles and aunts, 68 per cent of grandparents, but 135 per cent of psychotic parents. It could be expected that information about grandparents, uncles and aunts might be scarce, and data about siblings more readily available. For parents, information about peculiar behaviour is, as a rule, available in the case histories. We have probably been too inclined to consider depressive reactions or eccentric behavior as signs of psychoses. On the other hand, it may be, milder psychoses, not necessitating hospitalization, are more frequent among parents than among siblings. As will be seen from Part 4 of this Chapter, the parents have comparatively more suicides than siblings. They have also a greater proportion of affective psychoses. There is no reason why we should lose more hospitalized affective psychoses among siblings than in other relative groups. On the contrary, our experience was that we had lost less siblings with affective psychoses. Because of lower ages a considerable proportion of the siblings have, however, not yet passed the ages for risks of affective psychoses. We assume that these factors balance each other, so that the relative distribution of affective and schizo-phrenic psychoses should not be far from the true distributions.

When we compare the relative groups, the siblings have the most schizophrenic psychoses, the grandparents the most af-fective psychoses, and the parents take an intermediate position. Other investigations also indicate that parental generations have more affective psychoses than children (42, 89, 159, 162). This may be explained in several ways. The low fertility of schizo-phrenics would in a calculable time stop the propagation of simi-lar genetic loading. An increased fertility in persons with latent schizophrenic predispositions might counteract this factor, but this has never been proved. Then comes the possibility of progres-sive hereditary degeneration, which, according to modern genetic research, is very unlikely. The most likely interpretation is that af-fective and schizophrenic genetic predispositions overlap. Be-cause of reduced fertility (mainly due to low marriage rate), we would then find relatively more affective psychoses in the parental generations. We noticed that the married siblings had practically the same proportion of affective psychoses as the parents.

In Chapter IV the duration of illness before admission has been shown to be of great importance for the prognosis. In Table 43 this factor is correlated with the hereditary loading. (See table 43.)

TABLE 43

DURATION OF ILLNESS AND GENETIC LOADING

Case Histories of Relatives

Duration of Illness Prior to Admission in Probands	Affective Psychoses	Schizophrenics	Total
Less than 6 months	99	142	241
More than 6 months	67	125	192
Total	166	267	433

The table reveals that relatives of acute psychotics have a greater proportion of affective psychoses. Compared with the number of probands, the acute psychotics had also a greater number of sufficiently known psychoses than the insidious ones. Thus an acute onset of illness is associated with a favorable hereditary background, and possibly also with a greater constitutional predisposition to developing psychoses. In the experimental series of *Astrup,* the acute series had also more psychotic relatives than the chronic series, but these series are not quite comparable (9).

In the next table we present the types of hereditary loading in the five main outcome groups (see Table 44).

TABLE 44

CLINICAL OUTCOME IN PROBANDS COMPARED WITH RELATIVES

Probands Outcome	*Case Histories of Relatives*		
	Affective Psychoses	*Schizophrenics*	*Total*
Deteriorated schizophrenics	41	136	177
Improved schizophrenics	21	49	70
Recovered schizophrenics	24	40	64
Reactive psychoses	47	27	74
Manic-depressive psychoses	33	15	48
Total	166	267	433

From the table it is seen that those with a schizophrenic course of illness had considerably more schizophrenic relatives than the others (P < 0.001). The deteriorated schizophrenics had more schizophrenic relatives than the recovered ones (P < 0.05). Similar differences have previously been established by *Strömgren, Welner and Astrup* (9, 169). In contrast the recovered schizophrenics had more schizophrenic relatives than the affective psychoses (P < 0.001). As to affective or schizophrenic genetic loading, the manic-depressives and the reactive psychoses did not show essential differences.

In relation to the size of the proband materials, those with reactive psychoses had particularly few sufficiently known psychotic relatives. The deteriorated schizophrenics also had less psychotic relatives than the three remaining groups This may reflect that reactive psychoses are to a high degree dependent upon external factors, and that the worst outcome types of schizophrenia have less psychotic predisposition than the more favorable endogenous psychoses.

3. HEREDITARY FACTORS IN SUBGROUPS

For the various groups with a schizophrenic course of illness, the relatives have been coded in the same manner. The first

TABLE 45

GENETIC LOADING OF SCHIZOPHRENIC SUB-GROUPS

Types of Probands	Psychotic Relatives with Available Case Histories	Of Whom With Identical Pictures	Number of Suicides
Affect-laden paraphrenia	56	23	6
Schizophasia	20	7	4
Phonemic paraphrenia	13	0	0
Hypochondriacal paraphrenia	13	5	1
Confabulatory paraphrenia	1	0	0
Expansive paraphrenia	5	0	0
Fantastic paraphrenia	11	5	0
Incoherent paraphrenia	5	1	0
Autistic hebephrenia	3	0	1
Eccentric hebephrenia	21	2	7
Shallow hebephrenia	13	1	4
Silly hebephrenia	5	0	6
Periodic catatonia	57	26	1
Parakinetic catatonia	5	1	0
Speech-prompt catatonia	3	2	0
Proskinetic catatonia	3	2	0
Speech-inactive catatonia	4	0	2
Manneristic catatonia	8	0	1
Negativistic catatonia	1	1	1
Total	247	76	34

question was to what extent the relatives for each of the nineteen sub-groups resembled the probands. This may be seen from the following table (see Table 45).

In the total material 31 per cent of the relatives have the same clinical pictures as the probands. It is remarkable that the non-systematic schizophrenics have a greater proportion of relatives with the same defects than the systematic schizophrenics (P < 0.001). But we cannot confirm the opinion of *Leonhard* about a high degree of specificity of hereditary loading in the various schizophrenic subgroups (101). One reason for these discrepancies may be that we succeeded in obtaining a considerably greater number of case histories of psychotic relatives than *Leonhard*, and, in particular, of more affective psychoses.

Although all possible efforts have been made to analyze the case histories of the relatives, the information cannot be so detailed as for personally studied probands. The classification of relatives into subgroups has, therefore, only a limited validity. On firmer grounds is the classification of relatives into greater subgroups of slight and severe hebephrenic or paranoid defects, systematic and periodic catatonias, manic-depressive and reactive psychoses. The following table presents the findings for these broader subgroups (see Table 46).

From the table it is seen that slight paranoid defects as well as periodic catatonias, to a great extent, have relatives with similar psychoses. The systematic catatonics, and especially the hebephrenics, had a considerably smaller proportion of similar psychoses than the former groups. Probands with systematic catatonia had, however, mostly catatonic relatives, and fourteen of twenty-five systematic catatonics were relatives of catatonic probands. Ten of twenty-one hebephrenic relatives came from the hebephrenic proband groups. But the hebephrenic probands had thirty-two relatives with other types of psychoses, and sixteen of them were affective psychoses. The slightly deteriorated had more relatives with identical clinical pictures than the severely deteriorated.

The findings in the present sample were remarkably similar to those in the former series of *Astrup* (9). This comparison would support our assumption that comparisons between probands and

TABLE 46

TYPES OF SCHIZOPHRENIC DETERIORATION AMONG RELATIVES
OF SCHIZOPHRENIC PROBANDS

Probands	Case Histories of Relatives								
Clinical Groups	Slight Paranoid Deterioration	Severe Paranoid Deterioration	Slight Hebephrenic Deterioration	Severe Hebephrenic Deterioration	Periodic Catatonia	Systematic Catatonia	Reactive Psychoses	Manic-depressive Psychoses	Total
Slight paranoid deterioration	52	4	3	0	8	5	13	17	102
Severe paranoid deterioration	4	13	1	0	1	1	0	2	22
Slight hebephrenic deterioration	3	3	2	3	1	4	5	3	24
Severe hebephrenic deterioration	1	3	4	1	0	1	3	5	18
Periodic catatonia	9	1	2	1	26	5	4	9	57
Systematic catatonia	4	0	3	1	6	9	1	0	24
Total	73	24	15	6	42	25	26	36	247

relatives are rather valid, although a great proportion of case histories of relatives could not be obtained.

A comparison between the size of the proband materials and the number of psychotic relatives revealed that the hebephrenias had rather few psychotic relatives. The periodic catatonias had especially many psychotic relatives, which corresponds to the findings of *Leonhard* (101). The slightly deteriorated had comparatively more psychotic relatives than the severely deteriorated.

Leonhard has stressed the differences between systematic and non-systematic schizophrenias with respect to genetic background. Our data are summarized in Table 47 (see table).

We noticed that the probands with systematic schizophrenias had significantly more such psychoses than the non-systematic schizophrenias ($P < 0.001$), whereas the latter probands groups

TABLE 47

THE GENETIC LOADING OF SYSTEMATIC AND NON-SYSTEMATIC SCHIZOPHRENICS

Probands	Case Histories of Relatives				
Clinical Groups	Systematic Schizophrenia	Non-systematic Schizophrenia	Reactive Psychoses	Manic-depressive Psychoses	Total
Non-systematic schizophrenias	20	77	12	24	133
Systematic schizophrenias	63	25	14	12	114
Total	83	102	26	36	247

had more non-systematic schizophrenias ($P < 0.001$). Compared with the size of the proband material, the non-systematic schizophrenias had more sufficiently known psychoses than the systematic schizophrenias ($P < 0.001$). They had also more affective psychoses ($P < 0.05$).

The genetic loading of probands with a non-schizophrenic course of illness is presented in Table 48 (see table).

TABLE 48

TYPES OF SCHIZOPHRENIC DETERIORATION AMONG RELATIVES OF PROBANDS WITH NON-SCHIZOPHRENIC COURSE OF ILLNESS

Probands	Available Case Histories of Relatives								
Clinical Groups	Slight Paranoid Deterioration	Severe Paranoid Deterioration	Slight Hebephrenic Deterioration	Severe Hebephrenic Deterioration	Periodic Catatonia	Systematic Catatonia	Reactive Psychoses	Manic-depressive Psychoses	Total
Recovered schizophrenics	12	2	2	1	19	4	5	19	64
Reactive psychoses	13	2	3	2	6	1	32	15	74
Manic-depressive psychoses	8	2	1	0	3	1	6	27	48
Total	33	6	6	3	28	6	43	61	186

The table shows that probands with reactive psychoses had more than an average number of relatives with such psychoses (P < 0.001). The manic-depressives had an even greater proportion of relatives with similar psychoses.

There were in the whole recovered group fifteen relatives with severe and sixty-seven relatives with slight schizophrenic defects. The schizophrenic relatives of patients with a schizophrenic course of illness had a greater proportion of severe defects (P < 0.05). This shows that psychotics with a non-schizophrenic course of illness have not only more affective psychoses in their families, but also that their schizophrenic relatives tend to develop milder forms. There were twenty-five systematic and fifty-seven non-systematic defects. Thus there was a greater proportion of relatives with non-systematic schizophrenia than among relatives of chronic schizophrenics (P < 0.05).

Our next step was to analyze to which subgroups the various types of relatives belonged. The results of this analysis are presented in Table 49 (see table).

The typical manic-depressive psychoses have very few schizophrenic and mostly manic-depressive relatives. This is paralleled by the fact that for such psychoses a non-schizophrenic course of illness can be predicted with great probability (8).

Other groups with few schizophrenic relatives were querulent paranoia, reactive depression, confusional and other hysteric reactions. The relatives of these groups had altogether thirteen reactive, four manic-depressive and six schizophrenic psychoses. These psychoses all belong to the reactive group, and may with regard to heredity, as well as clinical course, be considered as the central reactive groups.

In Chapter II it was assumed that the querulent paranoia should be regarded as a non-schizophrenic group. The fact that these psychoses had only one close schizophrenic relative might support this assumption. The remaining paranoid groups had thirty-one relatives with affective and forty with schizophrenic psychoses. The majority of these paranoid probands had some typical schizophrenic symptoms. Thus they can clinically, as well as genetically, be considered as mixed affective-schizophrenic psychoses.

TABLE 49

THE GENETIC LOADING OF PSYCHOSES WITH A NON-SCHIZOPHRENIC
COURSE OF ILLNESS

Types of Probands	Suicides in Relatives	Reactive Psychoses in Relatives	Manic-depressive Psychoses in Relatives	Schizo-phrenic Psychoses in Relatives
Affect-laden paraphrenia	2	0	0	2
Anxiety-ecstasy psychoses	7	0	16	20
Sensitive delusions of reference	6	6	3	7
Querulent paranoia	0	2	1	1
Persecutory-affective psychoses	1	3	1	3
Stupor-confusion psychoses	0	1	1	8
Periodic catatonia	1	6	10	12
Motility psychoses	0	1	0	4
Confusional-hysteric psychoses	1	6	0	4
Other hysteric psychoses	0	0	0	0
Pseudo-neurotic and pseudopsychopathic schizophrenia	1	5	1	6
Depersonalization psychoses	7	5	6	8
Reactive depressions	2	5	3	1
Typical manic-depressive psychoses	17	3	19	6
Total	45	43	61	82

The clinical symptomatology of motility psychoses could only with difficulty be distinguished from periodic catatonias. According to the genetic loading there is even less reason to separate motility psychoses as a non-schizophrenic group. It is noticed that favorable outcome in periodic catatonia is associated with more affective loading than in those with a schizophrenic course of illness.

The pseudo-neurotic and pseudo-psychopathic schizophrenias had as many affective as schizophrenic psychoses among their near relatives. Genetically they were rather more schizophrenic than expected from the clinical analysis in Chapter II. According to the clinical analysis the depersonalization psychoses have more an affective than a schizophrenic character, and this is confirmed by the genetic loading: eight schizophrenic and eleven affective psychoses among relatives. In addition were seven suicides which also were probably due to affective psychoses.

We will try to illustrate the hereditary loading with some case histories. First we will present some cases where probands and relatives have the same clinical picture.

No. 16798 (case history reported on page 18) as an example of hypochondriacal paraphrenia had a brother, born 1912, who became insane in 1937 and afterwards was continually treated in a mental hospital. This brother was considerably depressed during the initial stage, but developed a clear-cut paranoid schizophrenia with marked feelings of passivity. Later on, auditory hallucinations and hypochondriacal sensations dominated the clinical picture.

The father was born in 1877. He became psychotic at the age of forty-two. After having been at home until 1928, he was a mental hospital patient up to 1954. Outstanding in the clinical picture were auditory hallucinations and hypochondriacal delusions. There is every reason to assume that these three patients all have hypochondriacal paraphrenia.

No. 16982 (case history reported on page 25), as an example of periodic catatonia, had a sister, born 1900, who became psychotic at the age of twenty-seven. Her disease started with a catatonic excitement, and she recovered from two catatonic episodes. But from 1932 until her death in 1945 she had to be continuously hospitalized. At the beginning of the psychosis the catatonic periods were combined with depression. Later on, aggressiveness and periods of violent psychomotor excitements were most characteristic. Another sister had been considered as nervous for several years until, at the age of fifty, she was admitted to a mental hospital. Her condition varied between catatonic excitation and stupor with negativism and rejection of food. At discharge there were no certain signs of a schizophrenic personality change. A brother was treated in Gaustad Hospital for a catatonic psychosis with violent psychomotor excitation, and had apparently complete remission. We think all the siblings have periodic catatonia, but the outcome varies from complete recovery to considerable deterioration.

No. 16481. Female, born 1897, was treated in Gaustad Hospital in 1947 for a depressive reactive psychosis, which occurred after the death of her husband. When re-examined in 1957 she had recovered completely and was socially well-adapted. A sister, born 1881, was from 1949 to 1958 treated three times in a mental hospital for reactive depression. Each time she recovered after a few months. The first psychotic period was precipitated by religious conflicts. A sister, born 1889, was treated for reactive depression in 1950. She thought that she had become depressed because the house seemed so empty after her son married and left home. A third sister, born 1885, was hospitalized for reactive depression in 1942.

No. 16400 (case history reported on page 40) as an example of reactive confusional hysterical psychosis, gave an example of three siblings with confusional reactive psychoses. We have thus clear-cut examples of the importance of the constitutional background in the predominantly psychogenic reactive psychoses.

Although the general rule was a tendency to similar psychoses in relatives, we were struck by the many exceptions to this rule. We will first present some cases with similarities in the acute stage, but variations in respect to outcome.

No. 15177. Female, born 1925, was a hysterical psychopath, who since 1941 had been hospitalized nearly once a year for short-lasting attacks of motility psychosis. There used to be violent psychomotor excitation combined with confusion. In 1960 she had just remitted from her last attack. A brother became psychotic. His condition shifted between psychomotor excitation and inhibition, and he could be classified as suffering from periodic catatonia.

Another brother also suffered from periodic catatonia, and after two years in the hospital was discharged as improved.

No. 17004. Male, born 1910, was treated in Gaustad Hospital in 1949 for paranoid schizophrenia. When re-examined in 1956, he lived on a very badly kept farm where he had been able to support himself. He had some ideas of reference, and speech was distorted in the manner which is typical of schizophasia. A brother, who also was treated in Gaustad Hospital, had the same clinical picture with a rather orderly behavior, and speech incoherence as the main symptom. A sister was treated in another mental hospital. She had a good working capacity, but speech was completely confused. We are inclined to assume that these three siblings all have schizophasias. During the initial stages of the psychoses there were strong affective traits in the clinical pictures. Two sisters had been treated in a psychiatric hospital for depressive reactive psychoses and had recovered. Both had some paranoid traits. One complained about being influenced by electric current and the other thought she was bewitched and transformed into a snake. The acute clinical pictures were not so unlike those of the three siblings who developed paranoid deterioration.

We had a great many families with mixed affective schizophrenic genetic loading. No. 16016. Male, born 1894, was treated in Gaustad Hospital in 1945 for manic-depressive psychosis. The clinical picture was dominated by manic elation and flight of ideas. In 1957 he was re-examined in his home and had a complete recovery. His father was treated in a mental hospital for manic-depressive psychosis between 1888 and 1890. During the hospital stay there was a shift between depression and manic excitement. He was discharged as recovered, and in 1923 was found to be mentally healthy. A brother, born 1892, also was hospitalized for manic depressive psychosis. But two brothers and one sister suffered from schizophasia and developed schizophrenic deterioration.

No. 14721. Male, born 1887, was classified in our follow-up as suffering from affect-laden paraphrenia. In the initial stage of the illness he was depressed and self-reproachful, with ideas of guilt, but he also had feelings of passivity and disturbance of symbolization. During later years strongly affective delusions of persecution and religious megalomania dominated the clinical picture. The grandfather had two attacks of a manic-depressive psychosis (case history not available). His mother suffered from manic-depressive psychosis. She had an involutional melancholia with a rather protracted course of illness. An aunt had had a melancholic depression at the age of thirty-two, and recovered spontaneously after six months at home. At the age of sixty-five she was admitted to a mental hospital for involutional melchancholia. A brother was hospitalized for melancholia and recovered completely. Two sisters suffered like the proband from affect-laden paraphrenia. One had religious megalomania.

No. 16293 in our follow-up was classified as affect-laden paraphrenia. Two sisters had periodic catatonias with a chronic course of illness. But the grandfather, an uncle and an aunt had manic-depressive psychoses.

The last three families mentioned illustrate that non-systematic schizophrenics often have relatives with affective psychoses. Furthermore, we notice a greater tendency to schizophrenia among siblings than in the older generations where all had affective psychoses.

In several families there was a mixture of affective psychoses and systematic and non-systematic schizophrenias. No. 16134. Female, born 1912, suffered from an anxiety-ecstasy psychosis. She was ecstatic, received commands from God, and heard voices speaking in her body. When re-examined in 1956 she had recovered completely, had a good job and was socially well-adapted. An aunt suffered from affect-laden paraphrenia, had persecutory delusions and ideas of reference. An uncle had eccentric hebephrenia with marked affective flattening, dysphoric periods, mannerisms and asked the characteristic stereotype question about being released from the hospital where he was treated. Furthermore, one cousin was hospitalized for eccentric and another cousin for silly hebephrenia.

No. 15064. Female, born 1903, became psychotic in 1933. She had an acute catatonic excitement and improved spontaneously so much that she could stay at home until she was admitted to Gaustad Hospital in 1941. She stayed in the hospital until 1948, when she died after leucotomy. During the hospital stay the patient periodically presented catatonic excitation. Between these periods there was a marked affective flattening and some negativistic traits. We are inclined to classify her symptoms as periodic catatonia. A brother was treated in another mental hospital for periodic catatonia with chronic course of illness. Another brother spent several years in Gaustad Hospital. Outstanding in the clinical picture was an affective flattening. He had several mannerisms, often knelt, went with closed eyes and poured water over his head. The total impression was one of an eccentric hebephrenia. A sister, born 1900, was treated in mental hospitals in 1940 and 1950 for a confusional reactive psychosis. She had complete remission.

No. 16778. Female, born 1915, was treated in Gaustad Hospital in 1948 for periodic catatonia. She had a second catatonic shift in 1953 and at re-examination presented only a mild defect. A brother was treated in Gaustad Hospital for several years and suffered from shallow hebephrenia. He was euphoric, had an outspoken affective flattening and was periodically hallucinated. A sister was treated in another mental hospital for a confusional reactive psychosis, and recovered completely.

No. 16497 (reported on page 116) could be clinically classified as a fantastic paraphrenia. A sister was treated in Gaustad Hospital for manic-depressive psychosis and had a classical mania with increased self-esteem and flight of ideas. She was re-examined in her home in 1957, and made a complete recovery with good social adaptation.

These cases may serve as examples of totally different psychoses in siblings. Another example of this is No. 15127. Female, born 1916. The clinical picture had the character of a depersonalization psychosis. When re-examined in 1956 the patient was mentally healthy and since discharge had married and had children. A brother, born 1912, had been treated for many years in Gaustad Hospital and suffered from phonemic paraphrenia. He heard voices coming from his head, which commented on his experiences in previous years.

4. SUICIDES AMONG RELATIVES

In the total material of relatives seventy-nine suicides were known. Compared with the series of *Dahl* and *Odegard* we have probably lost 25 per cent of the suicides (32). The manic depressives had twenty-six suicides among relatives, the reactive psychotics ten, and the schizophrenic psychotics forthy-three (9 for recovered schizophrenics). Compared with the size of the proband materials the affective psychotics had considerable more suicides than the schizophrenics (P < 0.02), and the manic-depressives again more than the reactive psychotics (P < 0.001).

Psychotics with a duration of illness of less than six months prior to admission had forty-seven suicides among relatives. Thus these with acute onset of illness had comparatively more suicides than those with an insidious onset.

The distribution between the various types of relatives gave eight grandparents, seventeen parents, twenty-three uncles and aunts, and thirty-one siblings. Thus the siblings have not only less affective psychotics, but also less suicides than the other relative groups (compared with the number of schizophrenics). Taking into consideration that suicides were more common among relatives of affective psychotics than those of schizophrenics, this should also be expected.

The next step was to investigate which subgroup had the most suicides. For the schizophrenic outcome groups (deteriorated and improved) twenty-nine of thirty-four suicides were relatives of probands with non-systematic schizophrenia and hebephrenic defects (see Table 45). These probands had fifty-two of the sixty-two relatives of schizophrenics with affective psychoses. This shows that the suicide risk of relatives of schizophrenic probands runs parallel to the genetic loading of affective psychoses. Our data correpond to those of *Leonhard* with respect to the many suicides among relatives of affect-laden paraphrenics and schizophasiacs. But the hebephrenics, according to *Leonhard,* had few suicides in the family (101).

In the non-schizophrenic outcome groups (affective psychotics and recovered schizophrenics), the typical manic-depressive psychotics revealed seventeen suicides. The central reactive group of querulent paranoia, reactive depression and hysteric psychoses had only three suicides (see Table 49). Of the remaining twenty-five suicides, twenty-two come in the groups of affect-laden paraphrenia, anxiety-ecstasy psychoses, sensitive delusions of reference, and depersonalization psychoses. These psychoses resemble the manic-depressives with regard to suicidal loading but have also many schizophrenic relatives. This is a common trait in the non-systematic paranoid schizophrenics, which they also resemble clinically.

In conclusion we find that the typical manic-depressive psychotic have most suicides in their families. The more other psychotic resemble them clinically, the greater is the genetic loading of suicides.

5. DISTRIBUTION OF FUNCTIONAL PSYCHOSES IN RELATIVES COMPARED WITH PROBAND MATERIALS

From the above it is seen that the clinical pictures of probands and relatives run rather parallel as a rule. In the following table we present the percentages of types of schizophrenic deterioration and affective psychoses for probands and relatives. We give also the data for the relatives of the experimental series of *Astrup* (9). The latter material consisted of schizophrenics, predominantly chronic cases, and very few recovered ones (see Table 50).

The table reveals that the follow-up cases and their relatives have practically the same distribution. The relatives have more periodic catatonias, which can account for the higher percentages of slight defects and the lower percentages of affective psychoses among relatives. According to the classification principles of relatives, it is probable that we may have coded systematically too many recovered psychoses as periodic catatonias. The reason for this is that in incomplete case histories of relatives, psychomotor excitation or stupor may be falsely interpreted as catatonic symptoms. It was also noticed that there were less hebephrenics among relatives than among probands.

The marked parallel between follow-up cases and their relatives indicates, however, that the lost hospitalized cases have hardly been of essential importance to our comparisons of outcome of illness in probands and relatives.

The relatives of patients in the experimental series had 45 per cent slight, 23 per cent severe schizophrenic defects and 32 per cent affective psychoses. The lower percentage of affective psychoses certainly reflects that the probands were schizo

TABLE 50

DISTRIBUTION OF FUNCTIONAL PSYCHOSES IN RELATIVES
COMPARED WITH PROBAND MATERIALS

Patient Materials	*Clinical Groups*							Total
	Slight Paranoid Deterioration	*Severe Paranoid Deterioration*	*Slight Hebephrenic Deterioration*	*Severe Hebephrenic Deterioration*	*Periodic Catatonia*	*Systematic Catatonia*	*Affective Psychoses. Including Recovered Schizophrenics in Follow-up Series*	
Percentages in follow-up series	24%	6%	8%	5%	10%	6%	41%	100%
Percentages among relatives of patients in follow-up series	24%	7%	5%	2%	16%	7%	39%	100%
Percentages among relatives of patients in experimental series	24%	10%	6%	3%	15%	10%	32%	100%

phrenic material. The great percentage of severe schizophrenic defects is not surprising, as 36 per cent of the probands had been classified as having longstanding defects of this type, and an additional 8 per cent were expected to develop these defects. In spite of these differences there was a fair parallel with regard to the distribution of the various types of schizophrenic defects.

The data of *Leonhard* show that in a psychiatric clinic the proportion of admitted affective psychoses was greater than in our series from a mental hospital. Careful community surveys, such as that of Bremer, reveal considerably more affective than schizophrenic psychoses. For schizophrenics certification as insane and institutionalization was necessary, whereas most of the affective psychoses had not been treated in a psychiatric hospital (23, 101). Also, according to the statistical data of *Ödegård*, schizophrenics are, as a rule, hospitalized (131). We would assume that deteriorated schizophrenics can represent only a small percentage of the unhospitalized, probably psychotic relatives, in our series.

Those patients with severe schizophrenic defects are unable, with few exceptions, to avoid hospitalization or family care as insane.

From the preceding considerations a more complete knowledge of unhospitalized probably psychotic relatives would have given a considerably lower percentage of severe schizophrenic defects, possibly more mild schizophrenic defects, and certainly more affective psychoses.

DISCUSSION AND FURTHER
RESEARCH PROBLEMS

1. IMPLICATIONS FOR DIAGNOSTIC CLASSIFICATION

Central problems of contemporary psychiatry are the international and national variations in principles of diagnostic classification. Psychoanalytic schools may argue that a diagnosis is only a label with small practical importance, and clinical symptoms merely superficial results of broken defenses, whereas the deciding factors are the psychodynamic mechanisms. From a different position the somatically oriented schools may consider symptomatologically based diagnoses as unspecific reactions to the most varied somatic etiologies. But still there are no proofs either for exclusively psychodynamic or somatic etiologies in the functional psychoses.

According to the school of *Adolf Meyer*, each psychiatric patient has his own personal reaction type. We have also the old conception of the unitary psychosis. Our material supports the unitary theory insofar as we are not able to separate distinct clinical entities, but have found all kinds of transitory forms between the typical cases. Within each clinical entity there are such great variations that one could agree with the principles of *Adolf Meyer* (105, 106).

There are, however, important reasons for a systematic classification with well-defined clinical disease entities. It is sufficient to refer to the importance of comparability in vital statistics, clinical research, and in the evaluation of new therapies.

As long as the etiology of the various types of functional psychoses is insufficiently known, there is considerable reason to follow the principles of classifying functional psychoses mainly on the basis of clinical symptoms. This was also done in the case of the bodily diseases before etiological factors were ascertained.

The present investigation indicates that it is most practical to classify functional psychoses on the basis of the symptoms in the acute stage, but having in mind the prognostic importance of the individual clinical factors.

In the case of schizophrenia a limitation of diagnosis to those with a chronic course of illness implies that the final diagnosis must be postponed for several years. From the initial symptoms we would not give absolutely definite predictions about the outcome of illness in the individual case. It seems most practical, to label those psychoses as schizophrenia, which according to clinical symptoms give a *great risk* of schizophrenic deterioration. With this concept of schizophrenia we could register 20 per cent recoveries. The chances of recovery varied from a few per cent in insidiously developing cases with late admissions to 50 per cent in acute schizoaffective subgroups.

On the other hand groups of affective psychoses could be differentiated, where on the basis of the initial symptoms a very small risk of schizophrenic deterioration could be predicted. The affective psychoses could be divided into one well-defined group of manic-depressive psychoses and a more heterogeneous group which we have called reactive psychoses.

Among acute psychoses originally diagnosed as manic-depressive, we had a schizoaffective group with approximately 50 per cent developing schizophrenic defects. This would mean that the psychoses with mixed schizophrenic-affective symptoms had about 50 per cent chances of recovery in the long run, whether they were diagnosed as schizophrenias, reactive or manic-depressive psychoses. On the other hand, we had the typical manic-depressive psychoses, where a non-schizophrenic outcome could be predicted almost with certainty (8).

According to our findings the diagnostic category of reactive psychoses has been too broad in Norway, including as it did a great percentage with schizophrenic outcome. If some typical schizophrenic symptoms were present, the risk of schizophrenic deterioration was so great, that these cases should have been included in the schizophrenic group.

It was possible to distinguish a great group of reactive psychoses without any typical schizophrenic symptoms, which could be catamnestically verified as non-schizophrenic. In the WHO classification this group is, to some extent, neglected. We find "paranoia and paranoid states", but *Ödegård* points out that the reactive depressions and psychoses with a symptomatology of confusion, excitement, etc., should also have a place in the system of psychoses (137). Recently *Fish*, after a thorough discussion, concluded that "paranoid state" is purely a label and not a diagnosis. He proposed that the paranoid states should be divided into schizophrenia, affective disorders, personality disorders and psychogenic reactions, and organic diseases (52). The nosological entity of involutional melancholia is also rather dubious. Depression in old age may, according to our material, be of a psychogenic as well as an endogenic nature, and is not essentially more atypical than the late schizophrenias compared with the juvenile forms. Genetic studies of German authors and *Stenstedt* indicate that the endogenic involutional melancholias as to genetic loading correspond very much to the classical manic-depressive psychoses (163, 164).

We would suggest that the term reactive psychoses should be a common diagnosis for most of the conditions called degeneration psychoses (22, 81, 158), phasic and cycloid psychoses (82, 101, 118), psychogenic psychoses (18, 54, 55), *"Abnorme seeliche Reaktionen"* (154), or schizophreniform psychoses. (In the Norwegian classification system the schizophreniform psychoses tend to be classified as reactive psychoses) (95). The common features in all those groups is a non-schizophrenic course of illness, neurotic or psychopathic predisposition and precipitation by more or less easily recognized exogenous factors.

From the American literature one receives the impression that our reactive psychoses would often be classified there as schizophrenias. For the evaluation of treatment it is important to remember that such psychoses even when untreated have a low risk of a schizophrenic course. This point of view is especially stressed by *Langfeldt* in the case of his "schizophreniform psychoses" (95) and by *Leonhard* for his "cycloid psychoses" (101).

The reactive psychoses cannot be sharply distinguished from the manic-depressive group, but some factors make the diagnosis of a manic-depressive psychosis more likely. Typical manic elation with flight of ideas is rarely found in our reactive psychoses, as are ideas of guilt and inferiority. Reactive psychoses with disturbances of consciousness can more easily be distinguished from manic-depressive psychoses than the depressive reactions. Reactive depressions are, however, more colored by life experiences and personality traits, whereas in the manic-depressive psychoses the clinical pictures are more uniform and relatively independent of personality factors. From our follow-up examinations it seems that the manic-depressive patients predominantly have syntonic personalities without neurotic traits, but suffer from periodic mood swings, sleep disturbances and other vegetative signs pointing to more fundamental biologic lability. Even this lability may contribute to the endogenous character that is in contrast to the more exogenous nature of reactive psychoses (8).

We have analyzed our follow-up material on the basis of the five observed outcome groups of deteriorated, improved and recovered schizophrenias, and reactive and manic-depressive psychoses. A further step would be to predict the outcome shortly after admission and make a follow-up after five years or more in order to ascertain to what degree the outcome actually can be predicted. Such a project we have already planned in collaboration with other Norwegian hospitals.

2. PROBLEMS OF DETAILED SUBGROUPING OF FUNCTIONAL PSYCHOSES

Within the five main outcome groups there were great clinical variations. We found it convenient to divide those with schizophrenic defects according to the schemata of *Leonhard* (101). We agree with *Leonhard* that the schizophrenic defects differ so much from each other that a differentiation may be useful. If symptoms of a certain defect type are recognized, it may also at an early stage be possible, not only to predict a schizophrenic outcome, but also the type of deterioration and the possibilities of social adjustment.

In particular it is important to be aware of *Leonhard's* "non-systematic schizophrenias." Such psychoses in the acute stages resemble very much the affective psychoses, and the majority of the schizophrenic defects falsely diagnosed reactive or manic-depressive psychoses were of this non-systematic type. The defects are usually slight with good chances of social adjustment and they constituted the majority of the improved schizophrenias. The non-systematic schizophrenics often lack affective flattening and autism, so that one can raise the question whether they have the clinical dementia praecox qualities described by *Kraepelin* (87).

We found most of our cases to present fairly typical pictures, but there were also many transitory forms. A deeper understanding of differences and resemblances probably must be expected through physiological research. To some extent *Astrup* has approached these problems with conditional reflex experiments (9).

The psychoses with a non-schizophrenic course of illness mostly belonged to the following groups: affect-laden paraphrenias, anxiety-ecstasy psychoses, stupor-confusion psychoses, sensitive delusions of reference, querulent paranoia, persecutory affective phychoses, periodic catatonia, motility psychoses, pseudoneurotic and pseudo-psychopathic schizophrenia, depersonalization psychoses, confusional and other hysteric reactions, and reactive depression and typical manic-depressive psychoses. These subgroups are overlapping within the three main groups of recovered schizophrenics, reactive and manic-depressive psychoses.

The reason for presenting prognostically favorable subgroups was mainly to point out more precisely how varied these reactions are. A detailed knowledge of such conditions implies the possibility of predicting a non-schizophrenic course at an early stage of the illness. Also it was remarkable how few patients with the characteristics of affect-laden paraphrenia or sensitive delusions of reference recovered as compared with those who had similar symptoms and developed schizophrenic defects.

The non-schizophrenic outcome groups were even less sharply distinguished from each other than the schizophrenic defects. The main reason for this is probably that no great and representative series of catamnestically verified benignant psychoses have previously been systematically analyzed. Another factor is that the subdivision of schizophrenic subgroups is based on the comparatively stable clinical pictures in the defect stages.

For the non-schizophrenic outcome groups the subdivision

had to be based on the shifting acute clinical picture. A simple symptomatological classification could not be used. The example of the manic-depressive psychoses clearly demonstrates how diametrically opposite syndromes can appear within a nosological unity. Analogous phasic shifts have been systematically studied for the anxiety-ecstasy, stupor-confusion and akinetic-hyperkinetic motility psychoses. These syndromes overlap very much and are similar to the manic-depressive psychoses not only with respect to clinical pictures, but also as to genetic loading and a basic psychic and vegetative lability. The other non-schizophrenic outcome groups are mainly characterized by their central syndromes. There was, however, some reason to assume that the hysteric and depressive reactive psychoses, to a great extent, represent merely variations with respect to the strength of the same reaction (8).

From the above it is obvious that much clinical research has to be done, until a satisfactory subdivision of the prognostically favorable functional psychoses is obtained.

3. THE DIAGNOSTIC AND PROGNOSTIC IMPORTANCE OF INDIVIDUAL CLINICAL SYMPTOMS

An important reason for the variations of diagnostic classification is the lack of agreement upon which particular symptoms a clinical diagnosis should be based. We have carried out a detailed symptom analysis and tried to define the symptoms precisely within a definite frame of reference.

On the basis of the literature we considered the following symptoms as typical schizophrenic: 1) Catatonic traits. 2) Emotional blunting. 3) Depersonalization (delusional type). 4) Passivity. 5) Disturbance of symbolization. 6) Haptic hallucinations. 7) Special types of auditory hallucinations: hearing the thoughts, conversation with voices, voices with comments on the patient's movements, and voices coming from the patient's own head or body. 8) Religious megalomania (such as Christ or prophets). 9) Corresponding non-religious megalomania (such as king, Stalin or Hitler). 10) Ideas of high descent. 11) Fantasy lover. 12) Fantastic ideas of jealousy.

The theoretical basis for selecting these symptoms was primarily data about their unfavorable prognostic significance.

Secondly, these symptoms could clinically be considered as mental automatisms (as opposed to psychodynamically understandable symptoms), and this assumption was supported by conditional reflex experiments. In these experiments all the above mentioned typical schizophrenic symptoms were associated with marked dissociation and disturbances of cortical-subcortical relationships (9).

The prognostically unfavorable catatonic symptoms clearly represent dissociations of movements which become isolated from their normal smooth connections. Analogies between catalepsia and liberation of postural reflexes point definitely towards a deficient cortical regulation of inborn reflexes (9, 148). The follow-up revealed that the violent purely hyperkinetic or akinetic symptoms gave comparatively good chances of recovery in acute psychoses. But the intermingling of excitatory and inhibitory disturbances which have a dissociative character, and are especially characteristic of the defect stages, were unfavorable. In the total material 30 per cent of those with catatonic symptoms recovered. But the recovered cases were all periodic catatonias or mixed paranoid-catatonic states, characterized by acute onsets and periodic courses of illness. These states may be pathogenetically quite different from the systematic catatonias, which predominantly develop insidiously and lead to the most severe types of schizophrenic deterioration.

Emotional blunting gave a particularly bad prognosis with 94 per cent developing schizophrenic defects. This symptom can clinically be considered as an insidiously developing dissociation of feelings. We have mainly registered as emotional blunting the defects of higher ethical and social feelings with consequent disturbances of more complicated patterns of behavior. Elementary affective responses, such as outbursts of rage, interest in food and also sexual activities (in particular, masturbation) may very well be increased. With this definition emotional blunting has been an important criterion for classifying patients as hebephrenics. The diagnosis of emotional blunting is, however, to a great extent dependent upon the intuition of the experienced examiner (the clinical flair). We would agree with *Fish* that one should be very cautious in registering an affective flattening (52).

Such cautiousness implies, however, that emotional blunting as a rule only can be established in longstanding psychoses.

Traditionally, *disturbances of thinking* have been considered as especially characteristic of schizophrenia. Incoherence is the classical sign of dissolution of associative connections, regarded as a basic symptom by *Bleuler* (19). But in our material incoherence was also very characteristic of definitely non-schizophrenic confusional psychoses. As many as 40 per cent with this symptom recovered. We are well aware that neologisms and speech disturbances of schizophasias and incoherent paraphrenias are very typically schizophrenic, but they are found clear-cut in the defect stages and then combined with clear consciousness. In the acute stages it was not possible to distinguish sharply between the incoherence of schizophrenias and non-schizophrenic psychoses. For the reasons mentioned above we would not define incoherence as a typical schizophrenic symptom. *Langfeldt* too has stressed that incoherence often occurs in other psychoses than schizophrenia (96).

Passivity was clearly prognostically unfavorable with 80 per cent developing schizophrenic defects. This symptom is considered by *Langfeldt* as characteristic of the schizophrenic process, and phenomenologically it has a classical character of mental automatism (30, 40, 41, 96, 97, 151). It is also basic in the schizophrenic symptom complex of thought withdrawal (*"Gedankenentzug"*) analyzed by *Schneider* and followers (4, 9, 52, 153).

Among patients with *disturbance of symbolization* only 19 per cent recovered. This symptom was central in the schizophrenic symptom complex of drivelling (*"Faseln"*) (153) and is practically always associated with the so-called primary delusions.

Depersonalization was considered by *Langfeldt* as a basic process symptom representing a dissociation of personality (94, 96, 97). We could confirm that delusional types of depersonalization were prognostically unfavorable. But depersonalization with insight into the lacking reality of the phenomena was the central syndrome of the non-schizophrenic depersonalization psychoses. When all types of depersonalization were included, 37 per cent recovered. We would add that the delusional types of depersonalization implied the patient's conviction of changes in his own person or surrounding, and were usually combined with feelings of passivity or other typical schizophrenic symptoms. In the depersonalization psychoses, there was only a feeling as if the person or surroundings were changed. The symptom was not combined with schizophrenic automatisms, but was associated with depression or anxiety, thus having more an affective than a dissociative character.

Hallucinations appear in all types of psychoses. The previously mentioned special types of auditory hallucinations, as well as haptic hallucinations, proved to be specially prognostically unfavorable with respectively 78 and 84 per cent developing schizophrenic defects. Cases with sexual hallucinations even had 87 per cent with a schizophrenic outcome. In the literature these symptoms have also generally been assumed to be associated with poor outcome (15, 52, 96, 113, 155). The haptic and special auditory hallucinations were mostly combined with passivity feelings, and thus were a link in the *Clérambault* syndrome, which is considered as processual schizophrenia (30, 40, 41, 96, 97, 151).

Primary delusions have been considered as characteristic of schizophrenia (71, 96, 97, 114). We found that the distinctions between primary and secondary delusions might often be rather subjective. The delusional content seems always possible to explain psychogenetically on the basis of psychodynamic theories (3, 16). We, therefore, found it most practical to analyze the delusions according to the types of psychotic content. An important reason for considering religious and corresponding non-religious megalomania, fantastic ideas of jealousy, delusions of fantasy lover or high descent as typically schizophrenic, was that such delusions had been considered as prognostically unfavorable in the literature (31, 43, 45, 60, 68, 85, 88, 107). In our material the following percentages developed schizophrenic defects: Fantastic ideas of jealousy 88 per cent, ideas of high descent 84 per cent, fantasy lover 82 per cent, non-religious megalomania 80 per cent, and religious megalomania 68 per cent. With exception of religious megalomania, these symptoms have in fact proved to be very strongly linked up with a schizophrenic course

of illness. The comparatively good prognosis of religious megalomania was due to a frequent occurrence in the acute schizoaffective states.

We would also stress that the typical schizophrenic delusions express great distortions of reality, seemingly related to
basic instinctive changes of self-evaluation and sexual feelings.
There seems to be a dissociation between conceptual thinking
and basic instincts. The typical schizophrenic delusions also tend
to be associated with schizophrenic mental automatisms of other
types, and in conditional reflex experiments they revealed marked
disturbances of unconditional reflexes, which depend upon subcortical centers (9).

Ideas of reference and persecutory delusions were common in
schizophrenia, but were also often found in the reactive psychoses. These delusions often represent exaggerated reactions to
hostile attitudes from other people or accentuated inferiority
feelings. When fantastic, such delusions give great risks of schizophrenic deterioration. The distinction between psychologically
understandable and fantastic delusions may often be difficult.
Furthermore, information about relations between actual frustra-
tion and delusions is scarce. The distinction between fantastic and
understandable delusions of jealousy may be subjective, but
those towards whom the jealousy is directed can as a rule give
reliable information about incomprehensible affirmations made
by the patients.

Though we were unable to single out schizophrenic types of
ideas of reference and persecutory delusions, hypochondria, ideas
of guilt and inferiority were, on the other hand, more characteristic of the affective than of the schizophrenic psychoses.

In conclusion, our analysis of delusions indicates that catamnestically, as well as theoretically, there is good reason to diagnose
schizophrenia when typical schizophrenic delusions are present.
Other delusions have only a limited diagnostic and prognostic
value.

Autism and ambivalence *Bleuler* considered as basic schizophrenic symptoms (19), but the evaluation of such symptoms is
rather subjective, it is difficult to define them precisely, and
several authors have pointed to the difficulties (15, 52). As our

symptom analysis was built mainly on case histories we were not able to carry out a reliable investigation of the prognostic importance of such symptoms.

Apart from the typical schizophrenic symptoms, several other individual clinical factors were strongly associated with a schizophrenic course of illness. Of great importance is the *duration of illness* before admission. In the group with less than six months' duration, 37 per cent have developed schizophrenic defects, whereas in the group with more than ten years, 88 per cent have done so. The importance of this factor is even more clearly realized, when considering the three schizophrenic groups. Of those with less than six months duration of illness 37 per cent recovered compared to only 5 per cent of the remainder. Thus in longlasting cases with schizophrenic symptoms the pathophysiological disturbances are seldom reversible.

Another important factor is the type of onset, which has been coded independent of the duration of illness. A really acute onset was very favorable with only 21 per cent developing schizophrenic defects. On the other hand, the illness took a schizophrenic course in 88 per cent of those with an insidious onset without periodic exacerbations. In the three schizophrenic groups the percentage of recovered gradually decreased from 45 per cent in those with acute onset without prodromal symptoms to 3 per cent in those with insidious onset without periodic exacerbations. An acute onset was, however, only exceptionally found in cases which had lasted more than six months prior to admission.

Among symptomatologically unfavorable factors could be mentioned the hebephrenic syndrome, mannerisms, blocking, and negativism. The hebephrenic syndrome is, however, by definition linked up with emotional blunting, and the others are rated as catatonic symptoms. Emotional blunting and catatonic symptoms are included among the typical schizophrenic symptoms.

Other factors strongly associated with a schizophrenic outcome of illness were a schizoid premorbid personality, low intelligence, precipitation by social misery or isolation, lack of precipitating factors, and such initial symptoms as change of personality, impulsiveness and tantrums, vagrancy, ideas of reference, jealousy and suspiciousness. These factors were, as a rule, associated either with insidious onset or late admission. As to schizoid personality and low intelligence, these factors may be more secondary to long-standing insidiously developing schizophrenic processes, than actual premorbid characteristics. Lack of recognized precipitating factors, or precipitation by social misery and isolation, is also more likely to be coded in long-standing or insidiously developing psychoses, than in acute psychoses developing in socially well-adapted persons. Finally the initial symptoms mentioned, and, in particular, change of personality, can, as a rule, not be established until the illness has lasted for a considerable period.

The diagnostic and prognostic importance of factors explicitly or implicitly implying an insidious onset or late admission should not be overestimated. Under these conditions there has, in fact, already been a considerable "duration of illness." A diagnosis of schizophrenia would, from the total clinical picture, generally be agreed upon by experienced clinicians, and poor chances of recovery reliably predicted.

The prognostic importance of the typical schizophrenic symptoms is also, to a great extent, dependent upon the time factor. It is sufficient to remember, that only 5 per cent recovered of those who had been psychotic more than six months prior to admission.

As to manic-depressive and reactive psychoses, several clinical factors showed statistically significant differences between these two groups. In the reactive psychoses the following factors were especially frequent: 1) Sensitive, hysteric or neurotic premorbid personalities. 2) Acute mental trauma, sexual conflicts, somatic diseases or childbirth as precipitating factors. 3) Absence of delusions. 4) Absence of thought disorder. 5) Absence of hallucinations. 6) Acute onset. 7) Short duration of illness prior to admission. 8) Confusion and hysteriform syndromes. 9) Intelligence below average.

The manic-depressives often showed these factors: 1) Cycloid of harmonious premorbid personality. 2) Somatic disease, childbirth or no precipitating factors. 3) Delusions of guilt or inferiority. 4) Flight of ideas. 5) Absence of hallucinations. 6) Acute onset. 7) Short duration of illness prior to admission. 8)

Pyknic body type. 9) Average or above average intelligence.

Important differences between these psychoses were the types of premorbid personalities as well as the greater tendency of reactive psychoses to be precipitated by acute mental trauma and psychic conflicts. The differences have been analyzed in more detail in our former publication (8).

We have systematically coded the individual clinical factors before following up the patients. Information form case histories may, nevertheless, have influenced our evaluation of the symptoms, as we could see if patients were discharged as recovered or psychotic. In order to control this bias, we shall in the new series code symptoms one month after admission, and re-examine patients after five years or more.

4. DISCUSSION OF MORTALITY AND SUICIDES

From the analysis of mortality it appeared that all functional psychoses had a high mortality. The high mortality was greater in the affective than in the schizophrenic psychoses. The high mortality found during the first years after admission was most pronounced in the manic-depressives. The psychotic state is thus associated with worse bodily health than in the general population.

It could not be decided from the mortality figures to what degree somatic factors had contributed to the psychotic breakdown, or to what extent the psychotic state had lowered the resistance against noxious factors. In the case of manic-depressive psychoses we know that there were often somatic precipitating factors. Many deaths from infections, however, may indicate a lowered resistance. Conditional reflex studies have revealed great changes of subcortical processes in the manic-depressives (9, 59, 77, 150). Possibly somatic disturbances of equilibrium induce changes of subcortical activity, which again weaken biological defence mechanisms.

Although the manic-depressive psychoses had greater mortality during the first four years and were more precipitated by somatic factors than the reactive psychoses, it is seen in Chapter V that the latter has a minor proportion of persons with good bodily health, and, in particular, more persons with psychosomatic diseases. This might imply that manic-depressives tend to have good bodily health, which is temporarily decompensated by dangers to life during psychotic periods. The reactive psychoses are more in a permanent state of lowered psychic and bodily health, and not in such great danger during psychotic periods. The permanently poor bodily health was associated with the highest mortality for the whole follow-up period.

The schizophrenics resemble the manic-depressives with respect to lowered resistance to infections. This may also be related to experimentally established disturbances of subcortical processes (9). Their low mortality from circulatory diseases may indicate a protection by their less intensive emotional reactions and their physical inactivity. Chapter V showed that the schizophrenics predominantly had good bodily health and seldom had psychosomatic diseases. These factors may also account for the fact that they have lower mortality than the affective psychoses.

Suicides were more common in the reactive than in the manic-depressive group, and the former also had slightly more attempts at suicide before hospital admission. Considerably more relatives of manic-depressives than of reactive psychoses had committed suicide. An explanation of this discrepancy might be that a constitutional predisposition plays a dominant role for the manic-depressives, whereas life stresses are the most important factors in the reactive psychoses.

It may be easier to protect the manic-depressives against themselves. They need only to be watched during the easily recognized psychotic periods, while those with reactive psychoses are more habitually in danger of reacting to life stresses by attempting suicide.

5. THE PROGNOSTIC SIGNIFICANCE OF SOCIAL FACTORS

Social factors were studied for personally re-examined patients only.

Before their illness the *reactive psychoses* showed a low working capacity (it was even less at re-examination), and their occupational level had declined considerably. Many belonged to the lower social class, and a great percentage had poor housing conditions. The majority were non-migrant and had married before admission. After admission they had the greatest percentage in the divorced or separated group. Many of them had children before, as well as after, admission. They were able to establish sexual relations over a long period. Before admission they usually lived with relatives, but in several cases the attitude of their hosts was hostile. At re-examination many lived alone.

Attitudes towards hospitalization were mostly appreciative, but many complained. Feelings of inferiority or social discrimination about having been a mental hospital patient were frequent. Many had psychosomatic diseases, and at re-examination practically one half had lowered enjoyment of life.

Before admission the *manic-depressive* group had better working capacity, higher social class level and better housing conditions than any of the other outcome groups. No group had as few with single marital status or no children before admission. They had also established sexual relations to a greater extent than the others over longer periods. Few lived alone and with a few exceptions, the relatives had positive attitudes towards them. Also they used to be appreciative of hospital treatment and felt essentially no uneasiness about having been a mental patient. Psychosomatic diseases were rare, and at re-examination the majority had satisfactory enjoyment of life. The general finding was that before admission the manic-depressives rated better with regard to social adaptation than the other outcome groups. The same was, to a great extent, the case at re-examination. In some aspects higher ages and circumstances connected therewith altered their favorable position.

The social characteristics of the manic-depressive psychoses were in good accord with the clinical findings, which indicates that these disorders have the character of a biological reaction, occuring in predominantly syntonic and harmonious personalities, and apart from giving an increased vegetative and psychic lability, the psychotic periods essentially leave the personality unchanged.

This contrasts with the reactive group, which had considerably less favorable social characteristics before admission, and, to a greater extent, were unfortunate in their living conditions after discharge. It is in good agreement with the clinical findings, which indicate that the reactive psychoses result more from psychic conflicts, or unhappy living conditions in the case of neurotically or psychopathically predisposed persons, whose abnormal character traits tend to be increased after psychotic periods.

The *recovered schizophrenics* resembled more the manic-depressives than the reactive psychoses in their social characteristics. It was noticed that in practically all social aspects they had as good, or even better, adaptation at re-examination than before admission.

Evaluated on the basis of social factors, the psychotic episodes of the recovered schizophrenics had left practically no residuals that hampered social adaptation. That is, compatible with the hypothesis that the psychotic episodes had the character of strong biological defence reactions of a protective nature, but were phenomenologically related to the manic-depressive reaction type. In fact the subgrouping of the psychoses with a non-schizophrenic course of illness showed a considerable overlapping between the manic-depressives and the recovered schizophrenics.

The recovered schizophrenics mostly resembled the non-systematic schizophrenics who, like the manic-depressives, have a tendency to a periodic course. They often shift between excitatory and inhibitory states, which can be difficult to distinguish from manic or melancholic phases.

The *chronic schizophrenics* have in most aspects, prior to admission, as well as after, more unfavorable social characteristics than the groups with a non-schizophrenic course of illness.

Deteriorated schizophrenics re-examined in Gaustad Hospital had, to a great extent, a low working capacity before admission. Predominantly they belonged to a lower social class, and the majority had poor housing conditions. Very few were married, and few had children, many lived alone or had no dealings with relatives.

Certain traits distinguished them from the chronic schizophrenics living outside mental hospitals. Before admission the latter had better working capacity, better social status and housing conditions, fewer persons living alone or estranged from their relatives. They were also more plaintive about hospitalization, feeling more social discrimination about having been a mental hospital patient, and they had less enjoyment of life. They had considerably fewer social complications, in particular, less aggressive behavior before, as well as after, admission.

The *improved schizophrenics* in most social aspects resembled the chronic schizophrenics who lived outside mental hospitals. Several factors indicated that this group had a marked tendency to isolation. Several were found in lodgings and hostels. At re-examination most were migrants, especially to Oslo, the only great town where they could "disappear" in the crowd. They had predominantly single marital status, few had children, most of them lived alone, and several had nothing to do with their relatives.

Apparently patients with schizophrenic defects succeeded to varying degrees in social adaptation, not only with regard to clinical but also with regard to social characteristics. The clinical analysis showed that the improved schizophrenics were predominantly of the non-systematic types, which often set in acutely. The chronic schizophrenics living outside mental hospitals practically all had slight schizophrenic deterioration, and mostly non-systematic schizophrenias. A great percentage of the chronic schizophrenias re-examined in Gaustad Hospital were severely deteriorated, and most of them were systematic schizophrenics, which, as a rule, develop insidiously.

It appeared likely that the deficient social adaptation of those staying in the hospital prior to admission was to a great extent secondary to insidiously developing schizophrenic personality changes. Their discharge from the hospital might also be prevented more by severe deterioration and impulsive aggressiveness associated with severe deterioration than by unfavorable social conditions for rehabilitation. Their satisfactory enjoyment of life may be a result of emotional blunting, whereas feelings of social discrimination and unhappiness in the chronic psychotics outside mental hospitals mainly indicate a preserved ability to react emotionally.

From the above it is obvious that clinical outcome is in different ways related to social factors. Our analysis of the data would rather indicate that these social factors to a great extent were secondary to prepsychotic personality traits, and the clinical course of illness. This does not exclude the importance of such factors in the causation, as well as the prognosis of functional psychoses. In the reactive psychoses the clinical, as well as the social data, indicate that there was an interaction of premorbid vulnerability and life stress. Even in the endogenous psychoses, which have the character of general biological reactions rather than psychodynamically understandable conditions, the clinical analysis mostly revealed external stresses precipitating the psychotic reactions. The first manic-depressive period was, as a rule, precipitated by external stress, whereas it was often difficult to set relapses in relation to major stress factors (8). When no external precipitating factors could be established in schizophrenics, the patients had, as a rule, been ill for a long period, and were too emotionally disturbed to be able to tell about sufferings they had experienced.

As to differences in premorbid personality traits, we could clearly demonstrate the effects of psychotic periods in reactive psychoses (8). We could also show that manic- depressives with cycloid personality traits in younger ages often had minor "nervous periods," and that the periods tended to increase vegetative and psychic lability (8). What was considered as prepsychotic personality might often be sequelae of minor manic-depressive periods.

The improved schizophrenics, as a rule, give a schizoid impression, and their social characteristics with their tendency to social isolation point in the same direction. From the case histories only one-fourth had been characterized as schizoid premorbid personalities previous to first admission. Very few of those with a non-schizophrenic course of illness were coded as schizoid. These data indicate that what we have coded as "schizoid premorbid personality" may actually have been long-standing signs of an undiagnosed schizophrenic process, corresponding to the personality changes of improved schizophrenics. We do not find it justifiable to assume that variations as to social characteristics are primarily due to differences in premorbid personality traits.

The influence of social factors on prognosis is probably so complex that it cannot be decided from our data to what degree they are of primary or secondary importance. We can only establish that social factors have an empirical prognostic value on a level corresponding to clinical symptoms or hereditary factors.

The problems of specific importance of social factors can probably be more successfully analyzed out from statistical studies of incidence and prevalence in various sociological groups. The material illustrates how difficult it is to decide if schizophrenics become ill because of unfavorable living conditions, or simply drift into the lower social strata as a consequence of the disease. Multifactorial transcultural comparisons may possibly give evidence concerning the importance of social factors to mental health (5).

6. THE PROGNOSTIC SIGNIFICANCE OF HEREDITARY FACTORS

In order to evaluate the influences of hereditary factors all available case histories of psychoses among siblings, parents, uncles, aunts, and grandparents have been studied. We have probably lost 20 per cent of the relatives treated in psychiatric hospitals for functional psychoses. There were no reasons to assume that the lost cases were a biased sample with regard to clinical outcome.

The proportion of schizophrenic psychoses was considerably greater among siblings than among their parental generation, and smallest among grandparents. This indicates that the constitutional predisposition to schizophrenia and to affective psychoses does not differ so much as most investigators of genetics think (73, 74, 101, 118, 163, 166). There are too many sources of error to venture a conclusion that an affective constitutional predisposition in following generations turns more schizophrenic. If corrected for marriage, we observed among married siblings practically the same proportion of affective psychoses as among parents.

The acute psychoses (with less than 6 months duration of illness prior to admission) had comparatively more psychotic relatives and a greater proportion of affective psychoses than the more insidiously developing psychoses.

In the varous clinical outcome groups the genetic loading was mixed everywhere. Those with a schizophrenic course of illness had significantly more relatives with schizophrenic and fewer with affective psychoses than those with a non-schizophrenic course.

Comparisons of systematic and non-systematic schizophrenias revealed that their relatives predominantly had similar psychoses. The schizophrenic relatives of patients with a non-schizophrenic course of illness were predominantly non-systematic schizophrenias, and few relatives had severe schizophrenic defects. The relatives of the systematic schizophrenias had fewer relatives with affective psychoses than those of the non-systematic schizophrenias. This supports the clinical hypothesis that non-systematic schizophrenia is a transitional group between systematic schizophrenia and affective psychoses.

Among the schizophrenic subgroups only the non-systematic schizophrenias and patients with hypochondriacal and fantastic paraphrenia had several relatives with the same clinical picture. It is remarkable that the non-systematic schizophrenias also, to a greater extent than the other schizophrenic psychoses, were precipitated by external stress. As only one-third of the relatives of schizophrenics had the same type of defects as the probands, we could not confirm *Leonhard's* hypothesis that the schizophrenic subgroups are genetically specific. There is a certain tendency to similar defects in relatives as in probands.

When the schizophrenic outcome groups and their relatives were divided into major groups of slight and severe defects, those with slight defects revealed a greater proportion of relatives with similar defects. Probands with slight defects had also comparatively more psychotic relatives than those with severe defects. We know that psychotic relatives are often not hospitalized. As this applies more to those with slight than those with severe defects, the differences may be even greater than our data indicate. In this study, as well as in a previous study of *Astrup*, it was possible to demonstrate that psychoses with slight schizophrenic defects were precipitated to a greater extent by external factors than those with severe defects. This was particularly the case with the slight paranoid defects and the periodic catatonias. *Astrup* also showed that the latter types, in particular, benefited from ataraxic drugs (9). This seems to show that exogenous and endogenous factors are supplementary rather than mutually exclusive.

Systematic catatonia represents the most severe type of schizophrenic deterioration, clinically, as well as in conditional reflex experiments (9). As patients with such defects have very few relatives with similar psychoses, other factors than constitutional predisposition must be more responsible for the poor outcome. This group appears rather "organic" in its clinical charactertistics. Precipitating psychic factors can seldom be established. The course of illness tends to be steadily progressive, and effects of somatic treatments are very slight or lacking (9, 101). The clinical defect symptoms are very parallel to neurological heredodegenerative disorders, with disturbances of circumscribed psychomotor systems. There may be better reasons for using this group than periodic catatonia to test the hypothesis of somatic factors in schizophrenia.

The recovered schizophrenics had significantly more schizophrenic and fewer affective psychoses among relatives than the reactive and manic-depressive groups. The relatives of the latter had predominantly similar psychoses. There is a fair parallel between clinical pictures and genetic loading. In particular the genetic findings seem to justify the theory that the clinical classification operates with a category of recovered schizophrenics, which should be separated from the affective psychoses.

The typical manic-depressive psychotics had mostly manic-depressive and very few schizophrenic relatives. This was paralleled with the clinical finding that for such psychoses a non-schizophrenic course of illness could be predicted with great probability (8).

Other groups with few schizophrenic relatives were querulent paranoia, reactive depression, and confusional and other hysteric psychoses. Most of their relatives had reactive psychoses. These psychoses all belong to our reactive group, and may with regard to heredity, as well as the clinical picture, be considered as the central elements of this.

According to the clinical analysis, depersonalization psychoses had more of an affective than a schizophrenic character. This was confirmed by the genetic loading. The pseudo-neurotic

and pseudo-psychopathic schizophrenics had as many affective
as schizophrenic psychoses among their relatives. Genetically they
were in fact "more schizophrenic" than could be expected from
the clinical analysis in Chapter II. The remaining types of functional psychoses had more schizophrenic than affective psychoses
among relatives, and mostly had some typical schizophrenic
symptoms in the clinical picture. Thus they could, clinically, as
well as genetically, be considered as mixed affective-schizophrenic psychotics.

In conclusion, the family background of our followed up
patients supports the unitary conception of functional psychoses.
The genetic loading is far from specific, and shows all kinds of
transitory groups. A great proportion of the psychoses among
relatives is clinically remarkably similar to those of the probands. This implies that the clinical syndromes are not incidental
manifestations of a basic disease, but have a certain biological
foundation. Paradoxically, the most hereditary types of functional
psychoses are also the most exogenous. Logically, it seems rather
reasonable that a great predisposition is easily manifested by
environmental stress, of whatever kind this may be. The significance of genetic loading for the course of illness seems to show
that a biological predisposition is more important than specific
psychodynamic factors to the prediction of outcome. In particular,
the schizophrenic deterioration cannot be interpreted in terms of
psychodynamic regression without neglecting important clinical
facts.

7. PATHOGENETIC MECHANISMS IN FUNCTIONAL PSYCHOSES

We have now defined the clinical, social and hereditary
characteristics of the three main groups of functional psychoses.
The next question is whether conclusions can be drawn concerning pathogenetic mechanisms.

In the reactive psychoses the pathogenetic mechanisms are
established more or less by definition: Neurotic or psychopathic
persons react with psychoses to external stress. The constitutional
predisposition to similar psychoses makes us sceptical about as-
suming specific etiological psychodynamic mechanisms. It could
be demonstrated that precipitating factors were of the most

varied types, predominantly psychic stress, but often combinations of psychic and somatic factors (8).

The experimental animal neuroses may serve as models for the reactive psychoses. Here we see that constitution plays a great role. Somatically weakened animals are predisposed towards neurotic reactions, whereas neurotic animals have more difficulty in enduring exogenous noxae such as infections or intoxications. Similar neurotic reaction types may also result from different types of overstrain of the nervous processes (9, 57, 70).

Astrup and others have shown that patients with reactive psychoses resembled neurotics in conditional reflex experiments. The disturbances of the higher nervous activity mainly affected cortical processes, and the influences of complex structures were great (9, 63). The importance of psychological complexes has been established by *Birnbaum* and others clinically and in association experiments (9, 17, 18). *Harzstein* showed that in reactive depression the psychodynamic complexes represent pathologically excited structures, inducing severe general impairment of cortical activity (63). In confusional hysteric psychoses the general disturbances proceed to a "black-out" of cortical activity. When the confusion is passed, the hysteric psychoses are rather similar to the depressions in their disturbances of the higher nervous activity. This corresponds to the clinical observation that these reactions to a great extent represent differences with regard to the strength of the reaction. The greater frequency of hysteric psychoses in younger people and the common relapses with depression some years after a confusional psychoses may be explained by the postulation of a general tendency to more violent reactions in younger people. With increasing age the nervous processes become progressively more inert. Experimental data indicate that paranoid reactive psychoses tend to be accompanied by inertness of the nervous processes, and this may partly explain the tendency for paranoid psychoses to occur at higher ages, the fact that they rarely relapse, and that there is a tendency for the paranoid attitude to persist (8, 9).

It should be stressed that much experimental and clinical research is needed in order to elucidate the pathophysiological differences of the various types of reactive psychoses. A better

physiological understanding of the formation of complex structures would not only imply experimental research, but also intensive penetration of the life history and subjective experiences
similar to that obtained in the psychoanalytically oriented research.

The clinical study of the manic-depressive psychoses revealed that these, in contrast to the reactive psychoses, had
more the character of general biological than psychodynamically
understandable reactions. The favorable social characteristics may
also fit in with this hypothesis. While the genetic loading shows
the importance of constitutional factors, precipitating factors are
usually found for the first attack of the psychosis (8).

A model for the manic-depressive psychoses may be some
experimental animal neuroses which, once evoked, tend to take
a cyclic course without the addition of external stress (70).
Clinically, we generally found it difficult to establish precipitating
factors for relapses of manic-depressive periods, and the disease
seemed to take its own course, mainly determined by biological
factors, such as heredity, sex and body type (8). *Astrup* and
others have shown that the manic-depressive psychoses tend to
present great disturbances of unconditional reflexes, which implies impairment of subcortical functions (9, 59, 77, 150). The
endogenous character of this disorder is probably associated with
this factor. It may be especially so with regard to the changes
of the vital feelings. The monotonous character of the symptoms,
independent of personality traits and life experiences, contrasts
strongly with the reactive psychoses. The experimental parallel
is the slight influence of complex structures in conditional reflex
studies of manic-depressives (9).

Such symptoms as tachycardia, mydriasis, constipation, loss
of weight, cessation of menstruation, alterations of sexual feelings,
dryness of skin, sleep disturbances, etc., have clearly the character
of somatic syndromes, as has been stressed formerly by *Kraepelin*
(87).

Biochemical research, though without reaching definite conclusions, in any case shows marked parallels between psychotic
phases and changes of metabolism. *Protopopov* has even claimed
to have found definite patterns of disturbances of higher nervous
activity and metabolism during remissions (150).

In the schizophrenic groups the symptoms could be considered as mental automatisms, which it was difficult to set in relation to personality structures or life experiences, or to interpret psychodynamically. The social characteristics of recovered schizophrenics were rather similar to these of manic-depressive, supporting the clinical assumption that these reactions are related reaction types, of a primarily biological nature.

The groups developing schizophrenic defects had rather unfavorable social characteristics before admission. It could not be decided to what degree these unfavorable social characteristics were primary. It seemed most probable that insidiously developing personality changes preceding the manifest psychosis were the most important factors. The external precipitating factors were mostly long-lasting psychic conflicts, so that it was difficult to decide whether the conflicts actually were consequences of psychotic personality changes rather than causes. Again, the clinical analysis revealed that an insidious onset, and other factors related to this, implied great risk of schizophrenic deterioration.

We are entitled to assume that the schizophrenic process, as a rule, is associated with an insidious development of certain mental automatisms. These automatisms could be interpreted clinically as dissociative phenomena related to disturbed cortical-subcortical interactions. The strong tendency of relatives to develop similar defects as the probands shows that constitutional factors play a major role in the schizophrenic deterioration. In particular, the considerable genetic homogeneity of certain subgroups can scarcely be explained out from enviromental similarities of probands and their relatives.

In another publication *Astrup* has analyzed in detail the connections between clinical symptoms and disturbances of the higher nervous activity in the group of schizophrenias (9). These and other investigations have corroborated the clinical hypothesis that the schizophrenic mental automatisms develop on the basis of dissociations and impairment of subcortical processes (9, 59, 77, 149, 174).

To some extent schizophrenia can be regarded as a sleep-resembling inhibitory state of a protective nature. In experiments this was paralleled with severe inhibitory disturbances of all levels of the higher nervous activity (9, 75, 147, 149, 174). Clinically,

Carl Schneider has made a special analysis of the resemblances between sleep and schizophrenia. The schizophrenic symptom complexes of desultoriness (*"Sprunghaftigkeit"*), thought withdrawal (*"Gedankenentzug"*), and drivelling (*"Faseln"*) correspond to various phases in normal falling asleep and awakening (153). In conditional reflex experiments *Astrup* has shown that each symptom complex was parelleled by characteristic neurophysiological disturbances of functions (9). The follow-up revealed that each symptom complex tended to develop different types of schizophrenic deterioration. This means that the acute clinical reaction type and therewith connected general disturbances of the higher nervous activity play a major role for the course of the schizophrenic process.

Bellak has presented a multifactorial theory of schizophrenia, considering deficient ego strength as most important in the chain of factors (15). Although this theory is logically sound, the rather nebulous psychodynamic notions do not seem to add any new facts to our knowledge of pathogenetic mechanisms of schizophrenia.

Fish has criticized psychoanalytic and existentialistic theories of schizophrenia, and we agree with his following statements: "The author's main objection to psychoanalytic theories of schizophrenia is that, like most other theories of schizophrenia, they gloss over many of the outstanding acute symptoms and do not take into account the great diversity of the chronic clinical pictures. There is also the basic objection to all Freudian theory that aspects of mental functioning, such as unconscious cerebration of self-awareness, are turned into fixed entities with some inner source of perpetual motion. To trace all schizophrenia symptoms to a loss of ego boundaries is to have a startling glimpse of the obvious. This disorder is so vague that it can account for everything and nothing at the same time." "It appears that where existentialist formulations are relevant they are merely repeating known facts or Freudian formulations in a more obscure and exotic manner" (52).

Our data indicate rather that schizophrenia is a general biological reaction to varied types of stress. Once the schizophrenic process has started, the further development may be explained from the principles of *autokinesis* and *schizokinesis* found in animal experiments by *Gantt* (9, 58). This would imply that the disturbances of the higher nervous activity and accompanying clinical symptoms tend to develop along certain neurophysiological paths relatively independent of the originally precipitating factors. The hereditary findings indicate that constitutional factors are of significance in this process.

8. PROBLEMS OF TREATMENT

Our follow-up demonstrates clearly that a knowledge of the course of illness is essential for the evaluation of the effects of treatment. In our series clinical factors have much greater importance in prognosis than the various types of somatic treatment.

Insulin coma or leucotomy in our series could apparently improve very little the prognostic outlook of schizophrenics treated with convulsive treatment. The outcome was considerably better in those with convulsive treatment than in those with no active somatic therapies, but the "untreated" cases were a selection of cases with prognostically unfavorable symptoms, so that our series did not allow any conclusions about favorable effects of convulsive treatment in schizophrenia. This problem could, however, be elucidated by comparisons with the previously followed up series of "untreated" patients from the psychiatric clinic in Oslo (94, 95). Our plan is to make a similar follow-up study of patients treated with ataraxic drugs during the acute stage. A further research problem would be to compare the long-trend possibilities of active somatic treatments to counteract various types of schizophrenic deterioration occurring in a material from the pre-shock era.

The "natural" course of illness may teach us much about the "physiological healing mechanisms." It was noteworthy that the improved schizophrenics predominantly had non-systematic schizophrenias. This seems to imply that it is difficult to reverse the schizophrenic process in the systematic schizophrenias, in spite of the somatic treatments they have received. An analysis of the effects of ataraxic drugs in chronic schizophrenics revealed that treatment had little effect on systematic catatonias, whereas systematic hebephrenic defects and, especially, slight paranoid defects and periodic catatonias could benefit very much. The improvement in the systematic schizophrenias only meant a reduction of symptoms, while the characteristic basic defects were essentially unchanged. The most striking effects were obtained in non-systematic schizophrenias (9).

Although the schizophrenic process was essentially unchanged in the systematic schizophrenias, the ataraxic drugs were able to reduce the patient's sufferings and normalize his behavior. Patients with systematic as well as non-systematic schizophrenias can have good possibilities of social adaptation outside a mental hospital, in particular, when the defects are slight. In our followed up cases a basic assumption for successful social adaptation was that psychotic ideas were encapsulated or modified in analogous ways.

Baumer, Mauz and *Markovskaya,* have also laid great emphasis on this "healing process" in followed up schizophrenics (13, 110, 111). Paranoid schizophrenics with slight defects often have good working capacity, good ability in verbal communication, well-ordered behavior apart from delusions, and slight neurophysiological disturbances in experiments. An important therapeutic problem should then be to fortify the physiological tendency to encapsulation of psychotic ideas. In the experience of *Astrup* this seems possible with ataraxic drugs, as well as group psychotherapy (7, 9, 10). In experimental studies *Harzstein* and *Astrup* have shown that the main effects of individual and group therapy was the modification of responses related to delusions (pathodynamic structures) (11). Patients who were clinically much disturbed and in experiments revealed severe disturbances of the higher nervous activity seemed to benefit little from group psychotherapy (7). This might indicate that psychotherapy has small chances of counteracting the basic schizophrenic process. That psychotherapy is not a procedure unattended by risk in the schizophrenias and schizophreniform psychoses could be demonstrated by a series of such cases admitted to Gaustad Hospital who had received intensive individual psychotherapy. Much research is still needed in order to ascertain the potentialities and the limitations of psychotherapy in the group of schizophrenias.

Our hypotheses of pathogenetic mechanisms point to some principles which might be taken into consideration when somatic treatment is used. We have first the problem of strengthening protective inhibition in acute schizophrenic reactions. Conditional reflex experiments indicated that ataraxic drugs acted through such mechanisms, in particular, with inhibition of subcortical processes (9). Clinically, as well as in experiments, the insidiously developing dissociative disturbances seem rather difficult to counteract. This implies that we should not be too convinced that future follow-up series during the tablet era will give better long term prognosis than the present series. The short time follow up of *Wirt* and *Simon* showed, in fact, that the routine administration of ataraxic drugs was less effective than a varied therapy based on clinical judgment (171).

The ataraxic drugs, just as convulsive therapy, still represent an unspecific therapeutic intervention. The most severe types of schizophrenic deterioration have, in the present series, in spite of all treatment, developed the same clinical picture as before the modern treatments (100). The possibility that they are less frequent cannot be excluded. This obviously shows the need for knowledge about the biochemical basis of schizophrenic deterioration and for specifically directed treatment.

In manic-depressive psychoses there is general agreement on the beneficial effects of convulsive treatment, in particular, to shorten depressive periods (14, 35, 152). The possibilities of preventing new attacks with treatment are apparently small (8, 35). In our series the long-term prognosis was practically the same in "untreated" cases as in those with convulsive treatment. With respect to social adaptation and the basic lability the disease apparently took its own course, mainly determined by biological factors, such as heredity, sex and body type (8).

The reactive psychoses, as far as they follow the criteria of *Jaspers* for psychogenic psychoses, should be completely cured (71). Our experience was, however, that they tended to have severe residuals, hampering an adequate social adaptation. For these patients the analysis of social factors points to a great need for after-care. The shock treatments have not given better long-term prognosis than for the untreated cases with respect to recoveries (8). The experiences of *Harzstein* may indicate that sleep therapy is more beneficial than convulsive therapy (63).

Whether the ataraxic drugs may improve the results is still dubious. In our opinion more emphasis on psychotherapy is important from a pathogenetic point of view, and conditional reflex studies of *Harzstein* support this assumption (63, 64). Our impression is that psychotherapy of such cases, is described too often in the literature as successful therapy for schizophrenics.

9. IMPLICATIONS FOR PREVENTION OF FUNCTIONAL PSYCHOSES

As to the possibilities of prevention of functional psychoses our follow-up offers many suggestions. Definite conclusions cannot, however, be drawn as long as the etiologies of the functional psychoses are to a great extent unknown.

From a genetic point of view it is important to notice that these with a non-schizophrenic course of illness have the greatest fertility. Furthermore, those with schizophrenic defects had very few children after hospital admission. Thus the bearing of children after the onset of a serious psychosis is quantitatively not a great problem, although we have tragic examples of psychotics unable to care properly for their children.

Probands with strong genetic loading of similar psychoses had a predominantly favorable outcome of illness. Those with severe schizophrenic deterioration had such a small tendency to similar psychoses in the family that no genetic precaution for the reduction of fertility could be recommended before the onset of illness.

We have several examples of massive genetic loading of functional psychoses. As a rule we found it impossible to explain why the functional psychoses should accumulate in these families. We are well aware of the empirical hereditary prognosis established by several authors (32, 73, 74, 163, 166). The figures of these authors cannot, however, give any reliable prediction in the individual case. For one half of our probands we had actually no psychoses in their immediate families, which could warn about risks of psychosis.

From the above we assume that prevention of functional psychoses must mainly be attacked from environmental points of view. The decisive factor here is the whole social structure within which man is living. *Astrup* has pointed to some basic factors, but we are far from having ascertained the complex influences of social environment upon mental health (5).

Our analysis of prognosis and social factors makes us face certain aspects. The schizophrenic defects are especially associated with unfavorable social characteristics, whereas the manic-depressive psychoses develop in spite of seemingly favorable living conditions. As to the basic social characteristics, there is nothing a psychiatrist can do, except bear in mind the importance of these factors. For individual mental hygiene some hypotheses may be set forth.

For the manic-depressive psychoses we must admit that nothing definite can be said about the possibilities of prevention. The prepsychotic personalities are, as a rule, harmonious and syntonic, although often cycloid. We had the impression that often these persons were too unconcerned about their own health. Warnings about a psychotic period were often disturbances of sleep, changes of weight and appetite and other vegetative functions. If there have been previous psychotic periods, it might be reasonable to regulate sleep and when possible to avoid over-burdening oneself during periods of psychic or somatic stress. This may also apply to persons with such psychoses in the near family.

For the prognostically favorable schizophrenias (recovered), the social characteristics were quite similar to those of the manic-depressives, and similar precautions might be taken. We should, however, bear in mind that these psychoses more often have sensitive, self-assertive or even schizoid personality structures and tend to become ill at younger ages. Interpersonal conflicts play a great role, and especially sexual conflicts. These psychoses represent also, to a great extent, reactions to existential conflicts or moral problems. The postpsychotic tendency to good social adaptation has very much the character of a maturation process. A possible method of prevention might be to support this process. Therefore, an awareness of puberty crises or related reactions even later in life might be counteracted by psychiatric counsel. The intensive psychotherapies, according to experiences from our hospital, might even add to the basic conflicts and imply risks of psychotic breakdown. One could also have in mind the possibilities of concentrating interests more on external activity than on internal problems. We would also stress that an early treatment is decisive for a favorable outcome. In this respect an important reservation is that the recovered schizophrenics are, to a great extent, pathogenetically different from those taking a chronic course of illness.

In the patient groups developing schizophrenic defects a schizoid prepsychotic personality and signs of social isolation were often noticed before the outbreak of the psychosis. We would point to the possibilities that educational steps in the direction of increasing social contacts and realistic attitudes might reduce the predisposition in schizophrenic reaction types. The precipitating factors were mostly long-standing conflicts in family or work, or even basically existentialistic discontent with the patient's own person or pattern of life. Attitudes and reaction tendencies may play an even greater role than the actual conflicts, which often could hardly be avoided. This implies a need for mental hygiene education about the interrelations between external stress and how to react to such stress. An extension of neuropsychiatric policlinics might also give practical guidance about how to solve existentialistic life problems.

In the reactive psychoses we found the most clearly defined connections between external stress and psychotic breakdown. These patients had mostly encountered severe blows in established sexual and social relationships. We had, however, a definite impression that sensitive predispositions exaggerated their reactions. In these patients more stoic attitudes may reduce the sufferings, whereas the schizophrenics rather lacked spirit to establish adequate sexual and social standards.

The clinical analysis revealed that in all types of functional psychoses personal conflicts played a major role. Poverty and social misery on the one hand, and war events on the other hand precipitated the psychotic reactions in only a few cases. The effects of social environment are, therefore, as a rule, manifested indirectly through the individual interpersonal relationships. We could demonstrate the social background through the variations in social characteristics of the various clinical outcome groups.

Educational books on mental hygiene have mostly laid the greatest stress on childhood experiences and education of children. There is a marked contrast between the overwhelming theoretical frameworks, based mainly on psychoanalytic theories, and the actual knowledge. Our data indicate that greater emphasis must be laid on preventing mental illness in the grown-up population. The life expectancy rates of functional psychoses vary according to various statistics from 5 to 10 per cent, and these psychoses predominantly manifest themselves a long time after puberty (5, 128). Our knowledge about the formation of predisposing personality traits is still too deficient for any preventive educational programs. One must start with the realization that certain constitutional predispositions and types of external stress are associated with risks of psychotic breakdown.

In the vast majority of our cases initial symptoms are observed a long time before the outbreak of the psychosis. If there is a genetic loading of psychoses or previous psychotic periods all types of initial symptoms indicated as far as possible avoidance of external stress. Certain symptoms, such as changes of personality, impulsivity and tantrums, vagrancy, unexpected preoccupation with philosophical or religious ideas were often observed in the schizophrenics. An awareness of these symptoms may contribute to earlier treatment, and eventually preventive counsel.

Our analysis of personality traits and types of conflicts indicates that preventive counsel must go along different lines for the various types of maladjusted persons in order to prevent psychotic breakdown.

Poor sexual adjustment and single marital status were found before admission in groups with a severe course of illness. We are far from recommending marriage as a solution of personal adjustment. Several of the patients with reactive psychosis were so immature that their marriages were dissolved, and sexual conflicts were often the reasons for psychotic breakdown. Contrastingly a marriage often seemed to have contributed to the stabilization of the recovered schizophrenics. We had, however, many patients who married without telling their spouses about the disease or were so mentally ill that they placed great burdens upon their families. Marriage counsel might help to elucidate to what extent marriage represents a protection or increased strain.

Our data also showed that stability in work, good housing conditions and being on good terms with relatives were prognostically favorable. Thus it seems that the more an adult individual is able to form a stable existence with regard to basic human needs, the smaller is the risk of severe mental illness. This broad conclusion could also be supported from the literature on psychiatric epidemiology (5). We still lack a synthetic analysis of the interaction of physiological, psychological, moral and economic factors that are important for mental health. This seems necessary in order to state fruitful problems for quantitative and objective verification.

Chapter VIII

SUMMARY AND CONCLUSIONS

The present study represents a follow-up of all first admissions for functional psychoses admitted to Gaustad Hospital during the years 1938 to 1950. The material consisted of 1,102 patients, and the follow-up was carried out during the years 1955 to 1960. Chapter I surveys how the patients were followed up.

As far as possible we aimed at a personal re-examination of discharged patients in their homes. This was rather time consuming, and we had to travel approximately 60,000 kilometers by car. An observation period of at least five years was regarded as necessary in order to establish the long-term prognosis. It was possible to trace all but two of the patients living in Norway. Some had left the country for unknown destinations and many were deceased within five years after admission. There remained 972 cases with an observation period of five or more years.

In Chapter II the catamnestically verified psychoses are divided into five main clinical outcome groups, namely 416 deteriorated, 117 improved and 131 recovered schizophrenics, and 102 manic-depressive and 206 reactive psychoses. A detailed clinical subgrouping is carried out of these five categories. Of the total material only 11 per cent were deteriorated schizophrenics staying in the hospital during the period of re-examination.

Chapter III surveys mortality and suicides and reveals a considerable excess mortality compared with the general population, particularly in the affective psychoses.

A detailed analysis of the prognostic importance of individual clinical factors is presented in Chapter IV. The analysis indicates that the diagnosis of schizophrenia should be limited to cases presenting clearly defined schizophrenic symptoms, which give a great risk of schizophrenic deterioration. Such symptoms were catatonic traits, emotional blunting, delusional types of depersonalization, passivity feelings, disturbance of symbolization, haptic hallucinations, special types of auditory hallucinations, religious megalomania and corresponding non-religious megalomania, ideas of high descent, fantasy lover and fantastic ideas of jealousy. Futhermore, a variety of factors, which were probably related to an insidious onset of illness or late admission to the hospital, gave a great risk of schizophrenic deterioration.

In Chapter V the social characteristics of personally re-examined patients are analyzed, before admission, as well as at re-examination. Before admission patients developing schizophrenic deterioration in practically all aspects had more unfavorable living conditions than the other outcome groups. The manic-depressives had in most aspects a good social background. From a social point of view the recovered schizophrenics succeeded better than the affective psychoses after discharge. They had good working capacity, many of them improved their occupational level, obtained better housing conditions, married and begot children.

In Chapter VI the genetic loading of the clinical outcome groups is analyzed by comparing the case histories of probands with the case histories of psychotic relatives. The relatives tended to have psychoses similar to those of the probands, but great differences as to genetic homogeneity were found in the various clinical subgroups.

Chapter VII deals with the theoretical implications of the findings, and further research problems are stated.

We are inclined to support the unitary conception of funcitonal psychoses, in as much as there were all kinds of transitory forms between the main diagnostic categories. Yet, even within the main diagnostic groups, the differences were so great that further subdivision seemed indicated for practical reasons. We have found the term "reactive psychoses" (of the official Norwegian nomenclature) quite useful for some clinical conditions which have neurotic or psychopathic predisposition or a non-schizophrenic course of illness and are clearly precipitated by external factors, mainly psychic stress. They differ in symptomatological, social and genetic aspects from manic-depressive psychoses, which have more the character of general biological reaction types, characterized by increased vegetative and psychic lability. Pathophysiologically, the reactive psychoses seem to have much in common with the neuroses.

The first attack of a manic-depressive psychosis was, as a rule, precipitated by external factors. When the disease had first started, it tended to take its own course, mainly dependent upon biological factors such as heredity, age, sex and body type. The endogenous character of the psychosis is mainly due to the somatic character of the reaction type, which in conditional reflex experiments was paralleled by marked disturbances of subcortical functions.

Our data indicate that schizophrenia is a general biological reaction to varied types of stress. Once the schizophrenic process has started, the type and extent of deterioration is dependent upon the constitutional background. The most exogenous types of schizophrenia reveal the greatest genetic homogeneity, and give predominantly slight deterioration.

Clinically, the schizophrenic symptoms had the character of mental automatisms. In the acute stages we could differentiate those reactions into the symptom-complexes of desultoriness, *("Sprunghaftigkeit")*, drivelling *("Faseln")* and thought withdrawal *("Gedankenentzug")*. These symptom complexes are to a great extent reversible. When symptoms characteristic of the defect stages described by *Leonhard* could be established, a chronic course of illness was practically certain. Distinction could be made between predominantly steadily progressive systematic schizophrenias and non-systematic schizophrenias with more periodic courses and fair chances of improvement and social remissions.

It is emphasized that the knowledge of the "natural course" of illness is of great importance to the evaluation of effects of treatment methods, as well as establishing rational principles of treatment.

On the basis of the follow-up data some suggestions for the possibilities of prevention of functional psychoses were set forth. It was especially pointed out how an evaluation of genetic loading, vulnerable personality traits, initial symptoms, and previous psychotic periods might be utilized for psychiatric counsel.

REFERENCES

1. Ackner, B. (1954): Depersonalization. *J. ment. Sci.*, 100, 838-872.
2. Aldrich, C. K. and M. Coffin (1948): Clinical studies of psychoses in the navy. *Prognosis. J. nerv. ment. Dis.*, 108, 142-148.
3. Arieti, S. (1955): Interpretation of schizophrenia. New York.
4. Arnold, O. H. (1955): Schizophrener Prozess und schizophrene Symptomgesetze. Wien.
5. Astrup, C. (1956): Nervöse Erkrankungen und soziale Verhältnisse. Berlin.
6. Astrup, C. (1957): Scandinavian literature on psychiatric genetics and epidemiology. *Acta psychiat. scand.*, 32, 399-424.
7. Astrup, C. (1958): Group therapy in a mental hospital with special regard to schizophrenics. *Acta psychiat. scand.*, 33, 1-20.
8. Astrup, C., A. Fossum and R. Holmboe (1959): A follow-up study of 270 patients with acute affective psychoses. *Acta psychiat. scand.* Suppl. 135.
9. Astrup, C. (1962): *Schizophrenia: Conditional Reflex Studies.* Springfield, Thomas.
10. Astrup, C. (1961): A note on clinical and experimental observations of the application of group therapy. *Internat. J. Grouppsychother.*, 11, 74-77.
11. Astrup, C. and N. G. Harzstein (1960): The influence of psychotherapy on the higher nervous activity of schizophrenics. *Internat. J. Grouppsychother.*, 10, 394-407.
12. Axel, M. (1955): Ten borderline cases. *Psychiat. Quart.*, 29, 554-587.
13. Baumer, L. (1939): Über geheilte Schizophrenien. *Z. ges. Neurol. Psychiat.*, 164, 162-178.
14. Bellak, L. (1952): *Manic-depressive Psychoses and Allied Conditions.* New York.
15. Bellak, L. (1958): *Schizophrenia.* New York.
16. Binswanger, L. (1957): *Schizophrenie.* Phullingen.
17. Birnbaum, K. (1912): Über den Einfluss von Gefühlsfaktoren auf die Assoziationen. *Mschr. Psychiat. Neurol.*, 32, 95-123 and 194-220.
18. Birnbaum, K. (1928): Die psychoreaktiven (psychogenen) Symptomenbildungen. In. Bumke, O. (edit.) *Handbuch der Geisteskrankheiten.* Bd. II, Berlin.
19. Bleuler, E. (1955): Lehrbuch der Psychiatrie. 9 Aufl. Berlin, Göttingen and Heidelberg.

20. Bleuler, M. (1940): Das Wesen der Schizophrenieremission nach Schockbehandling. *Z ges. Neurol. Psychiat.*, 173, 553-597.

21. Bleuler M. (1941): Krankheitsverlauf, Persönlichkeit und Verwandtschaft Schizophrener. Leipzig.

22. Bonhoeffer, K. (1907): Klinische Beiträge zur Lehre von den Degenerationspsychosen. Halle.

23. Bremer, J. (1951): A social psychiatric investigation of a small community in Northern Norway. *Acta psychiat.* (Kbh.) Suppl. 62.

24. Bremer, J. (1959): Einige Bemerkungen über dauernde Entfremdungserlebnisse und ihr Verhältnis zu den Schizophrenien. *II Internat. Cong. Psychiat.* 2, 142-147.

25. Brown, C. W., G. M. Carstairs and G. Topping (1958): Post-hospital adjustment of chronic mental patients. *Lancet*, 2, 685-689.

26. Campbell, J. D. (1953): *Manic-depressive Disease.* Philadelphia, London and Montreal.

27. Chase, L. and S. Silverman (1941): Prognostic criteria in schizophrenia. *Amer. J. Psychiat.*, 98, 360-368.

28. Christensen, R. (1961): Prefrontal lobotomy. A follow-up. (Nor.) Oslo. (monograph in manuscript).

29. Clarc, R. E. (1949): Psychoses, income and occupational prestige. *Amer. J. Sociol.*, 54, 433-440.

30. Clérambault, G. (1927): Psychoses a base d'automatisme et syndrome d'automatisme. *Ann. med.-psychol.*, 85, 193-236.

31. Dagonet, H. (1894): *Maladies Mentales.* Paris

32. Dahl, N. L. and J. Odegard (1956): On hereditary factors in functional psychoses. *Acta psychiat. scand. Suppl.*, 106, 320-335.

33. Dahlberg, G. (1933): Fertility among the mentally diseased. (Swed.) *Nord. Med.*, 6, 981-987.

34. Dayton, N. A. (1940): *New Facts on Mental Disorders.* Baltimore.

35. Dedichen, H. H. (1946): A comparison of 1459 shock-treated and 969 non shock-treated psychoses in Norwegian hospitals. *Acta psychiat.* (Kbh.) Suppl. 37.

36. Dunaif, S. and P. H. Hoch (1955): Pseudo-psychopathic schizophrenia. In. Hoch. P. H. and J. Zubin (eds.) *Psychiatry and the Law.* New York.

37. Dunham, H. W. (1959): Sociological theory and mental disorder. Detroit.

38. Eitinger, L. (1958):Psychiatric investigations among refugees in Norway. (Nor.) Oslo. Diss.

39. Eitinger, L., C. L. Laane & G. Langfeldt (1958): The prognostic value of the clinical picture and the therapeutic value of physical treatment in schizophrenia and the schizophreniform states. *Acta psychiat. scand.*, 33, 33-53.

40. Elgazina, L. M. (1954): About the Kandinsky syndrome with mental automatisms. (Rus.) *Z. Nevropat. Psihiat.* (Korsakoff.) 54, 707-709.

41. Elgazina, L. M. (1958): Clinical variations of paranoid schizophrenia. (Rus.) Z. *Nevropat. Psihiat.* (Korsakoff.) 58, 453-461.
42. Elsässer, G. (1952): Die Nachkommen geisteskranker Elternpaare. Stuttgart.
43. Esquirol, E. (1838): Des maladies mentales. Paris.
44. Essen-Möller, E. (1935): Untersuchungen über die Fruchtbarkeit gewisser Gruppen von Geisteskranken. *Acta psychiat.* (Kbh.) Suppl. 8.
45. Evensen. H. (1904): Dementia praecox. (Nor.) Oslo.
46. Ey, H. (1959): Unity and diversity of schizophrenia: clinical and logical analysis of the concept of schizophrenia. *Amer. J. Psychiat.*, 115, 706-714.
47. Faris, R. E. L. (1934): Cultural isolation and the schizophrenic personality. *Amer. J. Sociol.*, 40, 155-169.
48. Faris, R. E. L. (1938): Demography of urban psychotics with special reference to schizophrenia. *Amer. sociol. Rev.*, 3, 203-209.
49. Faris, R. E. L. and H. W. Dunham (1939): *Mental Disorders in Urban Areas.* Chicago.
50. Fellner, G. H. and P. L. Weil (1955): Low normal intelligence and schizophrenia. *Amer. J. Psychiat.*, 112, 349-353.
51. Fish, F. J. (1958): Leonhard's classification of schizophrenia. *J. ment. Sci.*, 104, 943-971.
52. Fish, F. J. (1962): Schizophrenia. Bristol, Wright.
53. Fünfgeld, E. (1936): Die Motilitätspsychosen und Verwirrtheiten. Berlin.
54. Färgeman, P. (1945): The psychogenic psychoses. (Dan.) Copenhagen. Diss.
55. Färgeman, P. (1946): Early differential diagnosis between psychogenic psychosis and schizophrenia. *Acta psychiat.* (Kbh.) 21, 275-279.
56. Galdston, I. (1947): On the etiology of depersonalization. *J. nerv. ment. Dis.*, 105, 25-39.
57. Gantt, W. H. (1944): *Experimental Basis for Neurotic Behavior.* London and New York.
58. Gantt, W. H. (1953): Principles of nervous breakdown: schizokinesis and autokinesis. *Ann. New York Acad. Sci.*, 56, 143-164.
59. Giliarovsky, V. A. (1954): Psychiatry. (Rus.) Moscow.
60. Gruhle, H. W. (1929): Psychologie der Schizophrenie. Berlin.
61. Hallgren, B. and T. Sjögren (1959): A clinical and geneticostatistical study of schizophrenia and lowgrade mental deficiency in a large Swedish rural population. *Acta psychiat. scand.* Suppl. 140.
62. Harris, A., I. Linker, V. Norris and M. Shepherd (1956): Schizophrenia. A prognostic and social study. *Brit. J. soc. prev. Med.*, 10, 107-114.
63. Harzstein, N. G. (1957): Studies of the nervous mechanisms in reactive depression and some types of treatment. (Rus.) Moscow Diss.

64. Harzstein, N. G. (1957): The influences of psychotherapy on the higher and autonomic nervous activity in anancastic neuroses and reactive depression. (Rus.) Nauch Konf. Dejat. Sign. Sist. Norm. i Patol. 24-25.

65. Haug, K. (1939): Depersonalization und verwandte Erscheinungen. In. Bumke, O. (edit.) *Handbuch der Geisteskrankheiten.* Ergbd. 1. Berlin.

66. Hoch, P. H. and P. Polatin (1949): Pseudo-neurotic forms of schizophrenia. *Psychiat. Quart.,* 23, 248-276.

67. Hollingshead, A. B. and F. C. Redlich (1958): *Social Class and Mental Illness.* New York and London.

68. Holmboe, R. and C. Astrup (1957): A follow-up study of 255 patients with acute schizophrenia and schizophreniform psychoses. *Acta psychiat. scand.,* Suppl. 115.

69. Inghe, G. (1958): Mental and physical illness among paupers in Stockholm, Copenhagen.

70. Ivanov-Smolensky, A. G. (1954): Essays on the pathophysiology of the higher nervous activity. Moscow.

71. Jaspers, K. (1948): *Allgemeine Psychopathologie.* Berlin and Heidelberg.

72. Johansen, E. (1958): A study of schizophrenia in the male. *Acta psychiat. scand.* Suppl. 125.

73. Kallman, F. J. (1938): *The Genetics of Schizophrenia.* New York.

74. Kallman, F. J. (1950): The genetics of psychoses. An analysis of 1232 index families. *Cong. internat. Psychiat.,* Paris, 6, 1-40.

75. Kameneva, E. N. (1957): Schizophrenia. The clinic and pathophysiological mechanisms of schizophrenic delusions. (Rus.) Moscow.

76. Kerbikov, O. V. (1949): Acute schizophrenia. (Rus.) Moscow.

77. Kerbikov, O. V., N. I. Otseretsky, E. A. Popov and A. V. Snezhnevsky (1958): *Textbook of Psychiatry.* (Rus.) Moscow.

78. Kielholz, P. (1959): Klinik, Differentialdiagnostik und Therapie der depressiven Zustandsbilder, Acta psychosomat. Doc. Geigy nr. 2.

79. Kiesler, F. (1952): Masked schizophrenia. Bull. Univ. Minn. Hosp. Med. Found. 24, 211.

80. Kinkelin, M. (1954): Verlauf und Prognose des Manisch-depressiven Irreseins. *Schweiz. Arch. Neurol. Psychiat.,* 73, 100-146.

81. Kleist, K. (1921): Autochtone Degenerationspsychosen. *Z. ges. Neurol. Psychiat.* 69, 1-11.

82. Kleist, K. (1953): Die Gliederung der neuropsychischen Erkrankungen. *Mschr. Psychiat. Neurol.* 125, 300-309.

83. Knight, R. P. (1953): Borderline states. Bull. Menninger. Clin. 17, 1-12.

84. Kohn, M. L. and J. A. Clausen (1955): Social isolation and schizophrenia. *Amer. sociol. Rev.* 20, 265-273.

85. Kolle, K. (1931): Die primäre Verrücktheit. Leipzig.

86. Kolle, K. (1931) Über Querulanten. Berlin.

87. Kraepelin, E. (1910): Psychiatrie. 8 Aufl. Leipzig.
88. Krafft-Ebing, R. (1888): Lehrbuch der Psychiatrie, Stuttgart.
89. Kraulis, W. (1928): Utersuchung dreier untereinander verwandter Stammbäume in sieben Generationen. Z. ges. Neurol. Psychiat., 114, 647-680.
90. Kretschmer, E. (1927): Der sensitive Beziehungswahn. 2 Aufl. Berlin.
91. Kretschmer, E. (1927): Über Hysterie. 2 Aufl. Leipzig.
92. Landis, C. and J. D. Page (1938): *Modern Society and Mental Disease.* New York.
93. Lange, J. (1928): Die endogenen und reaktiven Gemütserkrankungen und die manisch-depressive Konstitution. In. Bumke. O. (edit.) *Handbuch der Geisteskrankheiten.* Bd. 4. Berlin.
94. Langfeldt, G. (1937): The prognosis in schizophrenia and the factors influencing the course of the disease. Copenhagen.
95. Langfeldt, G. (1939): The schizophreniform states. Copenhagen.
96. Langfeldt, G. (1952): Some points regarding the symptomatology and diagnosis of schizophrenia. *Acta psychiat. scand.* Suppl. 80, 7-26.
97. Langfeldt, G. (1956): The prognosis in schizophrenia. *Acta psychiat. scand.* Suppl. 110.
98. Langfeldt, G. (1959): The significance of a dichotomy in clinical psychiatric classification. *Amer. J. Psychiat.,* 116, 537-539.
99. Leighton. A. H., J. A. Clausen and R. N. Wilson (1957): *Explorations in Social Psychiatry.* New York.
100. Leonhard, K. (1936): Die defektschizophrenen Krankheitsbilder. Leipzig.
101. Leonhard, K. (1959): Aufteilung der endogenen Psychosen. 2 Aufl. Berlin.
102. Levitt, E. E. (1958): On locating closed clinic cases for follow-up studies. *Ment. Hyg.,* 42, 89-93.
103. Lewis, A. (1936): Melancholia: prognostic study and case material. *J. ment. Sci.,* 82, 488-588.
104. Lewis, N. D. C. (1950): What do we know about dementia praecox? *Ment. Hyg.,* 34, 569-581.
105. Llopis, B. (1954): La psicosis unica. *Arch. Neurobiol.* (Madr.) 17, 3-41 and 141-163.
106. Llopis, B. (1960): Das allen Psychosen gemeinsame Axialsyndrom. *Fortschr. Neurol. Psychiat.,* 28, 106-129.
107. Malamud, W. and N. Render (1939): Course and prognosis in schizophrenia. *Amer. J. Psychiat.,* 95, 1039-1057.
108. Malzberg, B. (1940):*Social and Biological Aspects of Mental Disease.* New York.
109. Malzberg, B. and E. S. Lee (1956): *Migration and Mental Disease.* New York.
110. Markovskaya, M. (1953): Schizophrenic remissions in policlinic exam-

inations. (Rus.) *Z. Nevropat. Psihiat.* (Korsakoff.) 53, 200-202.

111. Mauz, F. (1930): Die prognostik der endogenen Psychosen. Leipzig.
112. Mayer, W. (1950): Remarks on abortive cases of schizophrenia. *J. nerv. ment. Dis.*, 112, 539-542.
113. Mayer-Gross, W. (1932): Die schizophrenie. In. Bumke, O. (edit.) *Handbuch der Geisteskrankheiten.* Berlin.
114. Mayer-Gross, W., E. Slater and M. Roth (1954): *Clinical Psychiatry.* London.
115. Meduna, L. J. (1950): Oneirophrenia: The confused state. Urbana, Ill.
116. Mitsuda, H. (1957): Klinisch-erbbiologische Untersuchungen der endogenen Psychosen. *Acta genet.* (Basel) 7, 371-377.
117. Müller, J. E. (1959): Die Entfremdungserlebnisse. Stuttgart.
118. Neele, E. (1949): Die phasischen Psychosen nach ihrem Erscheinungs —und Erbbild. Leipzig.
119. Nielsen, C. (1954): The childhood of schizophrenics. *Acta psychiat. scand.*, 29, 281-289.
120. Nielsen, J. M. (1948): Remarks on abortive cases of schizophrenia. *J. nerv. ment. Dis.*, 112, 539-542.
121. Nissen, A. J. (1932): Fertility of schizophrenics. (Nor.) *Nord. Med.*, 4, 929-934.
122. Norris, V. (1956): A statistical study of the influence of marriage on the hospital care of the mentally sick. *J. ment. Sci.*, 102, 467-486.
123. Norris, V. (1959): *Mental Illness in London.* London.
124. Ödegård, Ö. (1932): Emigration and insanity. *Acta psychiat.*, (Kbh.) Suppl. 4.
125. Ödegård, Ö. (1936) Mortality in Norwegian mental hospitals from 1916 to 1933. *Acta psychiat.* (Kbh.) 11, 323-356.
126. Ödegård, Ö. (1945): The distribution of mental diseases in Norway. *Acta psychiat.* (Kbh.) 20, 247-284.
127. Ödegård, Ö. (1946): Marriage and mental disease. *J. ment. Sci.*, 92, 35-59.
128. Ödegård, Ö. (1946): A statistical investigation of the incidence of mental disorders in Norway. *Psychiat. Quart.*, 20, 381-399.
129. Ödegård, Ö. (1951): Mortality in Norwegian hospitals 1926-1941. *Acta genet.* (Basel). 2, 141-173.
130. Ödegård, Ö. (1952): The excess mortality of the insane. *Acta psychiat. scand.*, 27, 353-367.
131. Ödegård, Ö. (1952): The incidence of mental diseases as measured by census investigation versus admission statistics. *Psychiat. Quart.* 26, 212-218.
132. Ödegård, Ö. (1953): Marriage and mental health. *Acta psychiat. scand. Suppl.*, 80, 153-161.
133. Ödegård, Ö. (1953): New data on marriage and mental disease. The incidence of psychoses in the widowed and the divorced. *J. ment. Sci.*, 99, 778-785.

134. Ödegård, Ö. (1956): The incidence of psychoses in various occupations. *Internat. J. soc. Psychiat.*, 2, 85-104.
135. Ödegård, Ö. (1957): Occupational incidence of mental disease in single women. *Living, conditions and health*, 3, 169-180.
136. Ödegård, Ö. (1958): A clinical study of delayed admissions to a mental hospital. *Ment. Hyg.*, 42, 67-77.
137. Ödegård, Ö. (1959): Psychiatric terminology. *II internat. Cong. Psychiat.*, 4, 278- 280.
138. Ödegård, Ö. and C. Astrup (1960): Internal migration and mental disease in Norway. *Psychiat. Quart. Suppl.*, 34, 116-130.
139. Ödegård, Ö. and C. Astrup (1960): The influence of hospital facilities and other local factors upon admissions to psychiatric hospitals. *Acta psychiat. scand.*, 35, 289-301.
140. Pasamanick, B. and P. H. Knapp (1958): Social aspects of psychiatry. Washington.
141 Pascal, G. R., C. H. Swensen, D. A. Feldman, M. E. Cole and J. Bayard (1953): Prognostic criteria in the case histories of hospitalized mental patients. *J. Consult. Psychol.*, 17, 163-172.
142. Peterson, D. R. (1954): The diagnosis of subclinical schizophrenia. *J. consult. Psychol.*, 18, 198.
143. Phillips, L. (1953): Case history data and prognosis in schizophrenia. *J. nerv. ment. Dis.*, 117, 515-535.
144. Polatin, P. (1948): Schizophrenia. *Med. Clin. North Amer.*, 32, 623-629.
145. Pollock, H. M., B. Malzberg and R. G. Fuller (1939): Hereditary and environmental factors in the causation of manic-depressive psychoses and dementia praecox. Utica, New York.
146. Polonio, P. (1957): A structural analysis of schizophrenia. *Psychiat. et Neurol.* (Basel), 133, 351-380.
147. Popov, E. A. (1941): The clinic and pathogenesis of hallucinations. (Rus.) Charkow. Diss.
148. Popov, E. A. (1949): The significance of the studies of Pavlov for psychiatry. (Rus.) *Nevropat. i Psihiat.*, 18, 46-51.
149. Protopopov, V. P. (1946): Pathophysiological foundations of a rational treatment of schizophrenia. (Rus.) Kieff.
150. Protopopov, V. P. (1957): Problems of the manic-depressive psychosis. (Rus.) *Z. Nevropat. Psihiat.* (Korsakoff.) 57, 1355-1362.
151. Renard, E. (1942): Le docteur G. Clérambault. Sa vie et son oeuvre. Paris.
152. Roth, M. (1959): The phenomenology of depressive states. *Canad. Psychiat. Assos. J.* Suppl. 32-54.
153. Schneider, C. (1942): Die schizophrenen Symptomverbände. Berlin.
154. Schneider, K. (1927): Die abnormen seelischen Reaktionen. In. Aschaffenberg, G. (edit.) *Handbuch der Psychiatrie.* Spez. Teil. 7 Abt. Leipzig & Wien.

155. Schneider, K. (1955): Klinische Psychopathologie. Stuttgart.
156. Schofield, W., S. R. Hathaway, D. W. Hastings and D. M. Bell (1954): Prognostic factors in schizophrenia. *J. consult. Psychol.*, 18, 155-166.
157. Schroeder, C. W. (1942): Mental disorders in cities. *Amer. J. Sociol.*, 57, 40-47.
158. Schröder, P. (1926): Über Degenerationspsychosen. *Z ges. Neurol. Psychiat.*, 105, 539-547.
159. Schulz B. (1940): Kinder manisch-depressiver und anderer affektiv-psychotischer Elternpaare. *Z. ges. Neurol. Psychiat.*, 169, 311-412.
160. Shepherd, M. (1957): A study of the major psychoses in an English county. Maudsley Mon. no. 3. London.
161. Slater, E. (1936): The inheritance of manic-depressive insanity and its relation to mental defect. *J. ment. Sci.*, 82, 626-633.
162. Slater, E. (1938): Zur Erbpathologie des manisch-depressiven Irreseins. Die Eltern und Kinder von Manisch-depressiven. *Z. ges. Neurol. Psychiat.*, 163, 1-47.
163. Stenstedt, Å. (1952): A study in manic-depressive psychosis. Clinical, social and genetic investigations. *Acta psychiat. scand.* Suppl., 79.
164. Stenstedt, Å. (1959): Involutional melancholia. *Acta psychiat. scand.* Suppl., 127.
165. Stockings, C. T. (1947): The depersonalization syndrome. *J. ment. Sci.*, 93, 63-67.
166. Strömgren, E. (1938): Beiträge zur psychiatrischen Erblehre. *Acta psychiat.* (Kbh.) Suppl. 19.
167. Ström-Olsen, R. (1949): Late social results of prefrontal leucotomy. *Lancet*, 1, 87-90.
168. Tietze, C., P. Lemkau and M. Cooper (1942): Personal disorders and spatial mobility. *Amer. J. Sociol.*, 48, 29-39.
169. Welner, J. and E. Strömgren (1958): Clinical and genetic studies on benign schizophreniform psychoses based on a follow-up. *Acta psychiat. scand.*, 33, 377-399.
170. Wing, J. K. (1957): Family care systems in Norway and Holland. *Lancet*, 2, 884-886.
171. Wirt, R. D. and W. Simon (1959): Differential Treatment and Prognosis in Schizophrenia. Springfield, Thomas.
172. Wortis, (1952): Psychiatric problems of minorities. *J. Nat. Med. A.*, 44, 364-369.
173. Zilboorg, G. (1956): The problem of ambulatory schizophrenia. *Amer. J. Psychiat.*, 113, 519-525.
174. Zurabashvili, A. D. (1958): The contemporary theories of schizophrenia (Rus.) Tiflis.

INDEX